POLL-ARIZED

POLL-ARIZED

Why Americans Don't Trust the Polls
And How to Fix Them Before It's Too Late

JOHN GERACI

HOUNDSTOOTH
PRESS

POLL-ARIZED

Why Americans Don't Trust the Polls — And
How to Fix Them Before It's Too Late

FIRST EDITION

ISBN   978-1-5445-2869-4 *Paperback*
       978-1-5445-2870-0 *Ebook*

FOR STEVE AND MATT...AND MOM

CONTENTS

"On almost every occasion when we release a new survey, someone in the media will ask, 'What is the margin of error for this survey?'

There is only one honest and accurate answer to this question—which I sometimes use to the great confusion of my audience—and that is, 'The possible margin of error is infinite.'"[1]

—HUMPHREY TAYLOR, FORMER
CHAIRMAN OF THE HARRIS POLL

1   Humphrey Taylor, "Myth and Reality in Reporting Sampling Error: How the Media Confuse and Mislead Readers and Viewers," *The Polling Report*, May 4, 1998, https://www.pollingreport.com/sampling.htm.

FOREWORD

—GEORGE TERHANIAN, PHD,
FOUNDER OF ELECTRIC INSIGHTS

On the night of November 7, 2000, I sat on Gordon Black's couch, my eyes fixed on his television as the election results streamed in. Gordon, Harris Interactive's CEO, reveled in placing big bets. And bet big he did that night: our team at Harris produced 72 election forecasts.

We referred to this night as the "largest polling experiment in history."

If we did well, it would validate Harris' enormous investment in the new enterprise of online polling. But if we did poorly, Harris' broader business would suffer. At 2:00 a.m., when I left Gordon's house, no one knew who the next president would be: the Bush-Gore race was too close to call (as we predicted). But we did not care: nearly every one of our predictions was on the mark. We were ecstatic.

Few pollsters have experienced such joy in the last three presidential elections. As John Geraci notes in *POLL-ARIZED*, pollsters' present situation is gloomy:

- Only 17% of US adults trust them.
- Just one in eight adults is confident pollsters will predict the next president correctly.
- Four in 10 adults do not believe pollsters should be entitled to explore critical societal issues if they cannot predict elections.

To make matters worse, today's low (<5%) survey response rates, possibly due to low trust, massively complicate the pollsters' task. Think of it this way: if the 95 nonresponders participated in surveys and gave different responses from the five actual participants, how would that affect predictions and all other data?

It is a scary thought. Pollsters desperately need an objective assessment and sharp suggestions to improve their predictions and solve their trust problem. John Geraci, a *master* survey researcher, is ideally suited for this task. It is what he does.

John and I first met about 25 years ago, a month after Gordon Black left me a voicemail inviting me to Rochester, New York, to learn more about his company. I had never heard of Gordon but quickly realized that he was the real deal. So I made my way to Rochester on Halloween day. An hour into our conversation, Gordon offered me a job on John's Youth and Education team. He also invited me back to meet John, who was out that day.

I returned to Rochester a week later. John is perceptive, and he detected a peculiar expression on my face as he described the hiring process for the role for which I was apparently interviewing. "Did Gordon offer you the job already?" he asked. "He did," I replied. Unflustered, John laughed and said, "I should have known!"

To make a long story short, I joined John's team and thrived—John always put me in a position to succeed. The team excelled, too. And why not? It mirrored John's personality: skilled, meticulous, committed, and trustworthy with a healthy dose of charisma.

His clients, then and now, hire him repeatedly because they know he will provide thoughtful suggestions and astute advice on complex business matters.

That is exactly what John delivers in *POLL-ARIZED*. He makes a strong case that pollsters need to simplify what they are doing and build trust. Then, perhaps, more pollsters can experience the joy Gordon Black and I experienced more than 20 years ago.

PREFACE

Like many people, I could not get to sleep on November 3, 2020. It was election night in America, and the presidential race between Donald Trump and Joe Biden remained unsettled when I finally turned in for the night.

I am sure many others also had trouble sleeping, not knowing who would be president. Maybe they were excited that their candidate seemed likely to win. Or perhaps they were fearful that the "other guy" might prevail.

On this night, a divided country united on one thing—the frustration of having no certainty about who our next president would be.

which makes predictions harder

I was wide awake for a different reason. As the night wore on, it became apparent that the 2020 polls were performing poorly. Pollsters, some of whom are friends of mine, were taking a beating on cable channels and Twitter. Reporters were misinterpreting the polls. Pollsters were getting defensive. Clouds were forming that seemed likely to threaten the credibility of polling going forward.

It was as if the election had become a referendum on pollsters' performance rather than the engine of democracy.

I am part of the market research industry. This field uses surveys and polls (and other methods) to guide decision makers in pretty much any organization you can imagine: *Fortune* 500 companies, nonprofits, even governments. When you see a new advertising campaign, a new product on store shelves, fresh features on products you already use, updated packaging, or an increase in the prices you pay, market research probably informed these changes. — *basically everything and anything*

Market research is big business. Estimates vary, but market research spending in the United States is likely in the $20 billion range.[2] US market research spending is larger than the whole economies of North Korea or Jamaica.

Pre-election polling is a small but resonant part of the market research field. It is the segment of market research most people know. The US presidential race is polling's Super Bowl.

It is a well-kept secret that although pre-election polling is the most public-facing aspect of what researchers do, it is hard to make money at polling. Most pollsters conduct polls because it helps build their brands and sell other, more profitable work. Others do so because they enjoy media exposure. Who does

---

2   "Market Research & Polling Services Industry Profile," Dun & Bradstreet, November 1, 2021, https://www.firstresearch.com/industry-research/Market-Research-and-Polling-Services.html.

not want to be on TV or a podcast discussing their views about the next election?

Polling failures reflect poorly on the broader field of market research. Pre-election polls have failed many times throughout history. They were struggling again in 2020, which is one reason why I could not sleep.

ethos: credibility

I am the president of a market research firm and have worked in survey research for more than 30 years. I have seen firsthand how the quality of data collected from surveys and polls has deteriorated over the past decade.

Survey research and polling is the only field I can think of where advances in technology over the past 20 years have reduced quality. We are lucky if 5% of those we invite to take a survey take part. We routinely toss a third or more of surveys from our datasets because we catch the respondent cheating.

My insomnia emerged from a worry that the performance of the 2020 polls would be a watershed event, not only for political polling but for the whole field of survey research. My profession is in trouble.

Many of us who work in market research kindled our interest in this field by studying opinion polling. Market research was created as a by-product of polling. It did not take polling's founders long to realize that polling for companies and brands was lucrative.

Trust in market research is dependent on the success of pollsters. Would recent polling failures herald the decline of a field that I had grown to love?

I had previous bouts with anxiety over pre-election polls. I fretted about the deteriorating quality of polling data after the 2016 election, when every credible pollster in the nation predicted Hillary Clinton would defeat Donald Trump.

Sometimes it is an everyday conversation that can enlighten a problem. My wife, Sue, and I stayed at an Airbnb in Florida in January 2017. The host, Dan, was an ardent Trump supporter. At one point, he asked me what I did for a living. When I replied that I was a survey researcher, our conversation quickly turned to why the polls failed to predict the 2016 election winner.

Listening to Dan, I realized the implications of the failure of 2016 pre-election polling for my company. Dan felt he could now ignore all polls—on issues, approval ratings, voter preferences, and more. Instead, he could trust the leaders he chose to believe in to tell him what America thought.

I found myself getting defensive. After all, the 2016 polls were not off by much. Polls missed by more in 2012 than in 2016, yet nobody seemed to care in 2012. The problem seemed that the 2016 polling errors resulted in an incorrect prediction, and our sensationalized media environment magnified these errors.

We can still trust polls to provide a sense of what the citizenry thinks about the issues, right?

Not according to Dan. He felt political leaders should ignore the polls because polls and pollsters are not trustworthy. Dan was dug into his positions. The damage was done. He would never trust a poll again.

A new term for this has been bandied about: *poll denialism*. Poll denialism is a refusal to believe any poll results because of polling's past failures. Survey researchers like me should be scared that this has a name.

Poll denialism is alarming, not just to the market research field but also to our democracy. Poll results are a vital way political leaders keep in touch with the needs of the public. Polls shape public policy. Politicians who ignore or deny them are ignoring public opinion. When the public ignores the polls, it sets a stage for autocracy.

George Gallup once remarked, "Polling is merely an instrument for gauging public opinion. When a president or any other leader pays attention to poll results, he is, in effect, paying attention to the views of the people."[3]

Gallup felt opinion polling was a high calling and noble field. Gallup named his master work on polling *The Pulse of Democracy*.

Market research remains tightly associated with political polling. My clients have not become as mistrustful of their market research as the public has become of polling, but they would be justified in having doubts. At least, they should be asking hard questions of research agencies such as my company.

Most of what market researchers study is more complex than pre-election polling. It is easy to ask someone if they will vote for candidate A or candidate B. Ever try to project the market

---

3   George Gallup, interview with NBC News, 1979.

size for a new groundbreaking product from a survey? Or to tell a marketer what the effect of a 10% price increase will be on sales? Or if it is worth the billion-dollar investment to buy a competitor?

These are complicated decisions that rest on the quality of market research findings. Researchers like me support these decisions every day.

Pre-election polling is the simplest type of survey research. If researchers cannot predict the next president, why should a client believe our market forecasts?

Market research is fantastic. It is a field I would recommend to any college student who has an analytical bent and likes to explore why people behave the way they do. Great researchers beautifully meld psychology, statistics, and business skill. The field abounds with intelligent, caring people.

For me, market research has been an excellent alternative to a career in academia. It is like being an academic researcher who works at 10 times the pace of a college professor on a much broader array of subjects. I have worked for hundreds of organizations in dozens of contexts and have had the sincere privilege of working for and with brilliant people for three decades.

But I am worried to the point of sleeplessness. I am afraid that election pollsters have mortally wounded the field I love. I am nervous that people's perception of pollsters will harm our democracy. And that pollsters will continue to mismanage the response to the abuse dispensed their way.

He is not happy.

I attended many polling events after the past six presidential elections. Each time, leading pollsters convened, shared data, and tried to figure out what happened to improve the polls for the next cycle.

These confabs quickly devolved into posturing, defensiveness, and salesmanship. Each time, they resulted in trade groups authoring white papers that defended pollsters' performance and made a few recommendations for future methodological tweaks. The result was even worse polls four years later.

Polling is not a field poised to fix itself.

Academics will investigate what is going on with the polls. But they proceed so glacially that implications they draw will be outdated by the time they are published. *Grip, read to fifth*

The media and talk show pundits will delve into what is wrong with the polls. A few will do an excellent job at a postmortem assessment. But the media are limited by format—the issues surrounding data quality for polls are too nuanced for a five- or ten-minute discussion and too dry or dull to draw viewership.

The polling failures of 2012, 2016, and 2020 should be a wake-up call.

Everyone should be concerned that we get the polls correct. I would like to see market research clients ask questions regarding data quality and potential errors and biases. I want them to value quality more. If the people who keep the polling firms afloat financially demand more quality from their market research projects, the polls will benefit.

I would like to see polling firms cast aside their defensiveness and discover the genuine reasons behind their mistakes and begin the process of rebuilding the public's trust in what they do.

I would like to see the American public realize that getting the polls right is central to our democratic way of life. Portraying public opinion is a critical way a citizenry keeps elected officials honest. Let us stop bashing the polls and instead have constructive conversations on how to make them work again.

These conversations will go a long way to putting a great industry back on the right path to become the pulse of democracy again. We need accurate polls now more than ever. We need to fix the polls before it is too late.

A NOTE ON THE CRUX POLL

We conducted a proprietary poll to determine how the public views polls and pollsters. My firm, Crux Research, fielded the study among 1,198 US adults and covered many issues discussed in this book. *a year old*

The Crux Poll took place online between October 6 and 17, 2021. Sampling and weighting were employed to ensure that respondent proportions for age group, sex/gender, race/ethnicity, education, and region matched their actual proportions in the US adult population.

This poll did not have a sponsor. Crux Research, an independent market research firm not associated with political parties, candidates, or the media, funded the poll.

A research summary and study data are available by request at info@cruxresearch.com.

[handwritten note] ↳ couldn't just include the data here??

CHAPTER 1

WHY POLLS MATTER AND WHY WE ALL SHOULD CARE THAT THEY ARE ACCURATE

ELIZABETH DOLE'S FAILED CANDIDACY SHOWS THE POWER OF THE POLLS

Elizabeth Dole was a potential Republican candidate for president in 2000. Although many knew her as the wife of former senator and presidential candidate Bob Dole, she had much going for her beyond her choice of husband. She had been Secretary of Labor, Secretary of Transportation, and head of the Red Cross.[4]

Dole was well spoken and well connected. She seemed poised to become the first woman with a realistic shot at the White House. Most pundits saw her as a viable candidate.

---

4   She would later be a US senator from North Carolina.

Yet, polls conducted before the primaries showed the nature of her support was problematic. Because she was the first serious female presidential candidate, her backing among potential male donors was low. (Even her husband, Bob Dole, stated that he would donate to John McCain, one of her competitors.)[5]

After doing poorly in early polls, Dole stumbled in fundraising and pulled out of the race without a voter ever having the opportunity to cast their ballot for her.

Dole likely would have had enough fundraising support to enter early primaries if not for these initial polls. She was a brilliant communicator, so who knows where her campaign might have gone from there.

The key contenders for the GOP nomination that year were George W. Bush and John McCain, both excellent politicians not known for their verbal prowess. Dole's chances looked solid on a debate stage.

Polling reflects public opinion and shapes it

Dole's failure to launch showed that polling not only reflects public opinion; it also shapes a presidential race. Early polls reinforced the systemic barriers that prevented women from becoming serious candidates at the time.

Even though Dole may not have won, she had a voice that deserved airing, and the early polls effectively "canceled" her. It would be another 16 years before a viable woman candidate for president would emerge.

Early polling limits the electability of lesser-known candidates. If the polling environment in 1992 was as it is today, Bill Clinton, who had little national

---

5   Richard L. Berke, "As a Political Spouse, Bob Dole Strays from the Campaign Script," *The New York Times*, May 17, 1999, https://www.nytimes.com/1999/05/17/us/as-political-spouse-bob-dole-strays-from-campaign-script.html.

awareness, might not have emerged as a contender. If polls were taken as early in 1976 as they are today, Jimmy Carter would not have stood a chance.

GOOD POLLS ARE AN ESSENTIAL
UNDERPINNING OF DEMOCRACY

Polls matter. A case can be made that polls are more critical ？ to democracy than elections. Although the election may be "the only poll that counts," opinion polls determine candidates' positions and who gets to run. Polls tether elected leaders to public needs between elections. We should all care deeply that we get the polls right.

Public opinion electrifies governmental power. Polling remains our best way to measure public opinion and convey it to leaders. In 1891, James Bryce wrote:

> America has shown more boldness in trusting public opinion, in recognizing and giving effect to it, than has yet been shown elsewhere. Towering over Presidents and State governors, over Congress and State legislatures, over conventions and the vast machinery of party, public opinion stands out, in the United States, as the great source of power, the master of servants who tremble before it.[6]

US elected officials are servants who bend to the will of public opinion, as measured by polls. They ignore the polls at their peril—as long as the public trusts those polls. When polls have problems, and politicians and citizens no longer trust them, it pulls the plug on the force driving our democracy.

---

6   James Bryce, *The American Commonwealth*, Vol. 2 (Indianapolis: Liberty Fund, 1888).

→ aided by slower government movement

There were no formal polls during the first half of the American democracy. Instead, the framers of the country designed a system where members of the House of Representatives would be counted on to represent the people's will.

the house acted as an opinion poll

There were spirited debates during the country's founding about how much power should be put in the hands of the people. Many advocated that the US president be chosen by a vote in the House of Representatives. US senators were only selected by popular vote in all states after the 17th Amendment was ratified in 1913 and took full effect in 1919. *cause one of the*
↳ 6 year terms had to end

It is no coincidence that the 17th Amendment spurred the first formal pre-election polls, which took place in the 1920s. The people finally had the power to choose all their representatives. Polling developed because politicians and the public wanted to know what we as a collective were thinking.

Americans probably did not trust their elected officials back then, and they certainly do not today. Our Crux Poll showed that just 12% of US adults currently trust Congress, and only 21% trust the federal government. We should not return to the days where the power derived from the people was channeled solely through elected officials. The polls are a much better conduit, if we can conduct them accurately.

(taken with a grain of salt)

ARE POLLS TOO INFLUENTIAL?

In his 1838 treatise *Democracy in America*, Alexis de Tocqueville worried that America's obsession with public opinion would result in the majority ignoring minorities and marginalized people. Tocqueville was not wrong. The influence of polling

interesting especially how early it was

resonates throughout our political process. As the above story about Elizabeth Dole illustrates, polls can favor the majority and reinforce marginalization—of women, unknown candidates, third parties, and so forth.

The force of public opinion can only work for everybody if we trust elected officials to correctly interpret the polls and punish them by voting them out of office if they do not.

Have polls become too influential? Their influence on power is undeniable. For better or worse, polls sway policy. Polls decide which candidates get to run, what they choose to talk about, and in many countries, when the elections take place. There are countries (such as the United Kingdom, Israel, Canada, and Japan) where the incumbent executive chooses the election date. They do so after careful consideration of what the opinion polls are saying. *—7 British Conservatives, for example, won't call an election when they're down 27%*

Polls directly influence the US presidential nominating process. Twenty-two individuals declared their candidacy for the 2016 Republican nomination. Fundraising success was the first screen to winnow the field for the primary debates, and early poll results affected each candidate's fundraising ability.

) There were so many 2016 Republican candidates that early debates were cleaved into two phases: a "JV" debate with the lesser-known candidates and a "varsity" debate with the better-known ones. *— how is that even fair?*

How was it decided which candidate was varsity debate worthy? By looking at polling data. Success in the polls caused Carly Fiorina to be promoted from the JV to the varsity stage after the initial Republican debates. The 2016 polls decided who became a serious candidate.

The failure of a US third party to emerge is directly linked to poll results.[7] The 2016 polls excluded third-party candidates, notably Libertarian Gary Johnson, from the debate stage, preempting any hope of his winning the presidency. The Commission on Presidential Debates determined that only candidates with 15% support in the polls would be allowed to debate. Johnson fell into a cycle where he could not meet the threshold, which caused him to be excluded from the debates, which were his best chance to improve his standing and meet the threshold.

Just as the polls effectively canceled Elizabeth Dole in 1999, the 2020 polls considerably influenced the Democratic field. The polls taken after each debate decided which candidates moved forward in the process.

Do pollsters hold too much sway in who gets support? I posed this question to a well-respected pollster. He felt the issue was more about how accurate the polls are. When pollsters do their jobs well, they tether politicians to the popular will and thus are a valuable contributor to democracy.

There is nothing wrong with accurately measuring the truth and communicating it. But there is great danger in inaccurately measuring public opinion.

In his book *In Defense of Public Opinion Polling*, Kenneth

---

7   Gordon S. Black and Benjamin D. Black, *The Politics of American Discontent: How a New Party Can Make Democracy Work Again* (Hoboken, NJ: Wiley, 1994).

Warren provides a compelling rationale for polling's importance to society:

> Not only do public opinion polls measure public opinion very adequately, better than any other method, but overall these polls serve American society quite well, especially American democracy, businesses, and consumers. Pollsters are not nefarious predators who prey on the American fabric. Pollsters are, excluding the always-present rotten apples, business professionals who try to uphold professional standards and ethics while dedicating themselves to doing the best possible job.[8]

But the bad apples have a lot of sway

Great leaders do not govern by public opinion, but they need to know where they stand. As a polling industry veteran wrote, "Leaders should regularly avail themselves of the tremendous wisdom bound up in the collective experiences and insights of the people they represent. And this is best done by virtue of polls."[9]

OUR CULTURE OF DISTRUST INCLUDES DISTRUST OF POLLSTERS

If polls are vital to our political democracy, why do Americans like Dan, my Airbnb host, have such deep distrust in them? According to the Crux Poll, just 17% of Americans trust pollsters.

It starts with the reality that not all pollsters do their jobs well. Many poorly designed polls are released. Even well-designed polls from good pollsters struggle to provide representative

---

8   Kenneth F. Warren, *In Defense of Public Opinion Polling* (Abingdon, UK: Routledge, 2018).

9   Frank Newport, *Polling Matters: Why Leaders Must Listen to the Wisdom of the People* (New York: Grand Central Publishing, 2004).

samples anymore. As pollsters, we contribute to democracy when we portray opinion accurately, but we do it a disservice when we do not.

The recent polling record is not good. Because of pollsters' questionable projections, polls have overtaken the story. This feeds into a cycle of mistrust, making it harder to do accurate polls in the future.

The media has played a significant role in creating distrust in pollsters. Today's media are starved for content. They will cover most released polls with little vetting of their sources. The media has contributed to pollsters being seen as "handicappers" for elections, rather than the voice of the electorate, as polling's founders intended.

Today's news organizations do not just cover poor-quality polls; they also create them. The media are often the funders and the driving forces behind the polls. Media-created polls are a case of journalists crossing a line to generate news rather than report information. Journalists commission polls to create content. They need something to talk about.

Fox News

Hopefully, the media will stop using polls to drive news and instead use them as they should—to reflect the electorate's opinions and provide nuance to the ups and downs of the campaign cycle. Polls should catalyze discussions but should not be part of the story.

POLLSTERS ARE SCARED

Today's pollsters are under fire. Because of the bad press they receive, they selectively publish their polls. Some notable polling organizations have chosen to stop polling out of a fear of being wrong. Our democracy is harmed as a result.

Control of the US Senate hung in the balance after the 2020 election. There were still two senatorial runoff elections to be held in January 2021 in Georgia. These were the most consequential senatorial races in the history of the United States, yet there was a lack of polling data for them. Pollsters were scared, and the risk to their brands of an incorrect call in Georgia was not worth it for them.

Georgia Runoff

A POLITICO story by Steven Shepard after the election declared stated:

> The public polls that drove so much of the news coverage ahead of November—and generated tremendous distrust afterward—have all but disappeared in Georgia, and they are set to stay that way; some of the most prolific, best-regarded media and academic pollsters told POLITICO they have no plans to conduct pre-election surveys in Georgia.[10]

Nate Silver of FiveThirtyEight tweeted:

> Pollsters are being chicken in Georgia, but this also reflects the incentives when they get way more shit for being wrong than

---

10   Steven Shepard, "Pollsters Disappear in Georgia with Senate on the Line," *Politico*, December 21, 2020, https://www.politico.com/news/2020/12/21/pollsters-disappear-georgia-senate-448854.

credit for being right. You're left with a deficit of high-quality polls in the state.[11]

Control of the federal government depended on the results of these Georgia elections. Polls performed well in Georgia during the 2020 presidential campaign. Yet, the best-known pollsters were scared of another polling miss and decided to sit the Georgia campaign out. They took their bats and balls and went home. This will continue to happen—good pollsters will shy away from pre-election polls.

WE SHOULD ALL CARE ABOUT THE POLLS IMPROVING

Quality polls are needed now more than ever. They can keep the loudest voices in the room in check. Good polls provide a safeguard against the establishment of autocratic leaders. They can paint a realistic picture of public opinion to elected officials, who derive their power from the consent of the governed.

Rather than divide the nation, polls can help unify it. David A. Graham write in *The Atlantic*:

> The real catastrophe is that the failure of the polls leaves Americans with no reliable way to understand what we as a people think outside of elections—which in turn threatens our ability to make choices, or to cohere as a nation.[12]

Polls have never been more vital to democracy—at a time when they are not trusted. *The Washington Post*'s slogan is "Democracy Dies in Darkness." The implication is that a free media is

11   Nate Silver (@NateSilver538), Twitter, December 28, 2020.

12   David A. Graham, "The Polling Crisis Is a Catastrophe for American Democracy," *The Atlantic*, November 4, 2020, https://www.theatlantic.com/ideas/archive/2020/11/polling-catastrophe/616986/.

essential to a democratic-style government. The same can be said of the polls.

It is no secret that we are living in a polarized time. People seem to no longer spend time with others who think differently than them. Polling remains one of the best ways to develop empathy—as the polls can show us what others think.

In his book *Polling Matters: Why Leaders Must Listen to the Wisdom of the People*, Frank Newport, senior scientist at Gallup, makes a strong case that polls are essential:

> The views of the people are often viewed as too ill informed, whimsical, and unstable to be considered on a regular basis. I believe this is a mistake. If the society is to prosper and move forward in an optimally adaptive fashion, it is vital that those charged with decision making take the people's views into account on as systematic and frequent a basis as possible.[13]

Unfortunately, Americans do not necessarily agree that polls currently reflect their voice. Crux Poll findings show that 44% of US adults agree with the statement, "Opinion polls are important to our democracy." Even fewer (38%) agree that "opinion polls are an important way we can keep our elected officials honest."

These findings from our poll trouble me. I began writing this book because I was worried that the recent performance of pre-election pollsters might harm my company's business. As I researched the topic more, I became concerned that the public's

---

13 Newport, *Polling Matters.*

lack of trust in polling data is a real threat to our democracy. People do not trust pollsters, which translates to a lack of concern about whether public opinion matters.

As pollsters, we need to change their minds. We need to rebuild trust. A failure of pollsters to develop and maintain trust with the public has caused Americans to doubt whether we can count on the polls to express the public's voice.

Polls are critical to the investments we make in America in all industry sectors—government, corporate, and nonprofit. We must restore the public's trust. Pollsters will not repair this trust until they predict elections reliably.

It should not matter whether your political views are liberal, conservative, or independent—everyone should see that polls play an essential role in a democracy. A world without polls is one where public opinion and thus democracy does not matter.

Polls are influential, matter, and are here to stay. Their influence is needed, as polls are our best way to keep leaders accountable between elections and keep special interests at bay. They are a vital underpinning of democracy.

CHAPTER 2

PRE-ELECTION POLLS HAVE NEVER BEEN AS ACCURATE AS POLLSTERS CLAIM

POLLING MISTAKES LAST FOREVER

High school and college history classes teach two classic polling blunders. In 1936, the *Literary Digest* predicted Alf Landon would defeat Franklin Roosevelt for the presidency in a landslide. In 1948, Gallup and others erroneously forecast that Thomas Dewey would defeat Harry Truman.

} LoL

The 1936 election signaled the end of the *Literary Digest* (the most popular magazine in the country) and the nascence of Gallup's reputation, as Gallup confidently predicted a Roosevelt victory. Roosevelt won all but two states.

History teachers rarely mention that Gallup's 1936 final poll was off by seven points, well beyond its sampling error.[14] Why don't the history books recall that this poll was imprecise? Because Gallup predicted the correct winner.[15]

Twelve years later, in 1948, the *Chicago Daily Tribune* published its legendary "Dewey Defeats Truman" issue. This headline was based on a Gallup poll. It was accompanied by polling's best-remembered image: a picture of a grinning, newly reelected President Truman holding the newspaper announcing his defeat.

As Richard Wirthlin wrote, "That image is seared into the psyche of any good pollster." I have seen this picture displayed in dozens of offices in polling organizations. It reminds today's pollsters of their fallibility.

Gallup was not the only pollster who was sharply criticized for the 1948 polling miscall. On the air the next day, a CBS commentator handed Elmo Roper an abacus[16] and suggested that it might improve his future work.

---

14 Sampling error happens when projecting a representative sample to a larger population. It can be calculated, and it is expected that about 5% of all polls should end up being outside their sampling error. For most pre-election polls, sampling errors are between 3% and 5%. Gallup's 1936 poll polled tens of thousands of people and would have had a sampling error of well less than 1%.

15 "Gallup did miss the call by seven percentage points, yet he at least picked FDR to win, something the public remembers more than the percentage point margin."—Warren, *In Defense of Public Opinion Polling.*

16 "Roper gave it to the Roper Center for safe-keeping, to remind the industry that, though the polls may falter from time to time, those in the field should always strive to improve upon the art and science of survey research." "History of the Roper Center," Cornell University, accessed February 15, 2022, https://ropercenter.cornell.edu/about-center/history-roper-center.

EARLY POLLING BLUNDERS SET BACK RESEARCH
AND POLLING FOR A GENERATION

The causes of these two missteps are largely irrelevant to today's polls. Polling methods have evolved since these early days, and the field of statistics has advanced considerably.

Yet these two blunders, which occurred before the construction of the interstate highway system, the widespread adoption of television into US households, and the beginning of the Korean War, continue to loom large over the polling field. They still contribute to the perception that polls can go very bad.

These stories are told as amusing anecdotes. But they are not funny: these miscues set back the adoption of market research by America's emerging postwar economy by decades.

It was not until the late 1970s and early 1980s that market research became part of US business school curricula, companies integrated research into their marketing processes, and US research spending took off.

Missteps like those in 1936 and 1948 reverberate. Researchers should be concerned that our field will face something similar based on the performance of the 2016 and 2020 pre-election polls. A lack of trust in polling can take generations to change.

THE 1936 AND 1948 POLLING DEBACLES
WERE NOT OUTLIERS

Pollsters promote a revised history of the performance of pre-election polls. The accepted narrative in the polling industry is that 1936 and 1948 were disastrous years for pollsters but that pollsters learned from these mistakes, did an excellent job with pre-election polls until 2016, and the 2016 polls were not all that bad.

These three elections are hardly the only times pre-election polls missed the mark. There have been 22 presidential elections since 1936. Nine of these elections had polling miscalls, including five out of the six elections since 2000.

Below is a summary of sizable pre-election poll miscues in the modern era:[17]

- **1936:** The *Literary Digest's* straw poll, considered the gold standard in polling, predicted Alf Landon would rout Franklin Roosevelt by 370 electoral votes to 161. Roosevelt won in a landslide, with 523 electoral votes to 8 for Landon. This poll was off by almost 20 points in its national popular vote projection.
- **1948:** Major pollsters, including Gallup, Roper, and Crossley, concluded that Thomas Dewey would defeat Harry Truman by about five points. Truman won by 4.5 points, meaning most major pollsters were off by nearly 10 points. This polling debacle launched a periodic trend of austere committees studying "what is wrong with the polls."[18]
- **1952:** Reeling from the 1948 debacle, the major pollsters equivocated in their comments before the election. Pollsters predicted a narrow Dwight Eisenhower win but were

---

17   An excellent discussion of preelection polling problems in these elections is provided in Joseph W. Campbell, *Lost in a Gallup: Polling Failure in US Presidential Elections* (Oakland: University of California Press, 2020).

18   Frederick Mosteller, "The Pre-election Polls of 1948; Report to the Committee on Analysis of Pre-election Polls and Forecasts," *The American Journal of Sociology* 56, no. 2 (1950): 200–2, https://www.journals.uchicago.edu/doi/abs/10.1086/220705.

careful to cover all bases by stating that Adlai Stevenson had clear paths to victory. Gallup predicted a tie going into election night. Eisenhower won in a landslide, by 11 points, and by 442 to 89 in the electoral college. The year 1952 is not recalled as a polling miscue because headlines did not declare "Stevenson Defeats Eisenhower." Yet, Gallup's polling error was slightly higher in 1952 than in 1948.

- **1980:** Most national pollsters projected the race between Jimmy Carter and Ronald Reagan as being close. Gallup's final poll had Reagan with a one-point lead. The result was a decisive victory for Reagan, who won by more than eight points and achieved a commanding electoral college victory, 489 to 49. According to author W. Joseph Campbell, "No prominent pollster came close to suggesting a rout was in the making."[19] The campaigns' internal pollsters, particularly Richard Wirthlin, Reagan's pollster, came much closer to the final vote tally than the better-known national polling brands.

- **2000:** Pre-election polling errors were at about their historical average in 2000. Most major pollsters either declared the race a tie or close. But the polls throughout the campaign were unstable. Of 19 final polls, 14 had Bush winning the popular vote, with five of those having his lead at five points or more. Two of the 19 polls had the correct result, a slim popular vote victory for Gore. The rest had the race as a dead heat.[20]

- **2004:** This election was devastating for exit polls, which forecast a John Kerry victory over George W. Bush in most battleground states. Pollster John Zogby was quoted saying

19 Campbell, *Lost in a Gallup*.

20 Michael W. Traugott, "Trends: Assessing Poll Performance in the 2000 Campaign," *The Public Opinion Quarterly* 65, no. 3 (2001): 389–419, https://www.jstor.org/stable/3078826.

that Kerry would win an electoral college victory of 311 to 213. Pre-election polls were in line with their historical accuracy or inaccuracy, and 2004 is remembered for a failure of exit polls to accurately forecast to journalists on Election Day.

The end of Gallup and Pew; Birth of 538

- **2012:** This election became the final straw for the Gallup Organization, which decided to stop doing pre-election polling following their miss in this election. Pew Research Center also stopped conducting pre-election polls after 2012. Gallup forecasted a one-point victory for Mitt Romney over Barack Obama. Obama won by about four points. This cycle was a coming of age for modeling firm FiveThirtyEight, which got all 50 states' predictions correct after getting 49 states right in 2008.
- **2016:** Donald Trump defeated Hillary Clinton on the most surprising election night since 1948. Although the polls were off by their historical average, most major polls were off in the direction of overpredicting Clinton's vote. Not a single credible pollster or data journalist gave Trump more than a passing chance to win the election.
- **2020:** The 2020 polls were off by even more than in 2016, with most overpredicting the size of Joe Biden's victory over Donald Trump. As in 2016, the polling bias was in the direction of underestimating Trump's vote total.

Better economy Better polls

Except for 1980, the pre-election polls were accurate in their predictions from 1952 to 1996. This era was characterized by soaring economic and population growth in America. Most people were reachable for polls by landline telephone, response rates were high, and Americans trusted both pollsters and institutions.

The election cycles of 2000 to 2020 happened in an era when

internet polls came of age, response rates to polls plummeted, and telephone-based research became expensive and less reliable. Five of the six presidential elections in this period had questionable polling projections.

HOW GOOD OR BAD ARE THE POLLS?

The public and media perception is that pre-election polls have been dreadful in the past two presidential cycles. In efforts to fix these perceptions, polling insiders are repeating historical mistakes. They are tweaking their methodologies, making them overcomplicated and incomprehensible, and not pursuing the core problem facing their organizations: the lack of trust in pollsters and polling data. Pollsters are fixing the wrong problem.

Before delving into what has gone wrong with the polls and how to fix them, it is helpful to begin by answering an essential question: how good or bad are the polls?

This is the question that dogged me for weeks after the 2020 election. The media was berating the pollsters, yet the pollsters claimed the polls were not all that bad. What was the truth?

It was hard to know who to trust, so like any good researcher, I decided to get the data and see for myself. I deliberately stopped looking at what others were writing about the polls and attempted to assess the pre-election polls' performance in an unbiased fashion. What I found is what led me to write this book.

Let us begin factually. This is only fair. We need to ignore the conversations, which can be loud and often uninformed, and do our own analysis to answer the question of how good or bad the polls genuinely are.

There are four questions to consider to gauge pre-election polls' accuracy.

1. WHAT ARE WE TRYING TO PREDICT?

The popular vote does not decide US presidential elections. Winners are determined by the electoral college, with each state allocating its vote to electors, who vote for president. There have been 59 presidential elections in US history. The popular vote winner has lost the election five times by failing to secure enough votes in the electoral college.[21]

Using "number of electors" to judge pre-election polls is challenging because few pollsters attempt to predict electoral votes. The underlying reason has to do with the economics of the polling business. Forecasting the electoral vote would involve polling state by state or at least conducting polls in all potential toss-up states. The money is not there to do this.

State-level polls (of varying quality) are rarely conducted comprehensively by a single, reputable pollster. Many observers posit that poor-quality 2016 state-level polls led to the polling woes of that cycle.

Instead of electors, we can use a measure that pollsters consistently gather. The *predicted national popular vote percentage* is the most straightforward measure to use. More specifically, the

---

21 Electoral college winners of these elections were John Quincy Adams (1824), Rutherford B. Hayes (1876), Benjamin Harrison (1888), George W. Bush (2000), and Donald Trump (2016).

gap in the predicted percentage between the two major candidates is a crucial metric to use. These data are available and are what many researchers use when judging the polls. So, for example, in 2020, Joe Biden beat Donald Trump by 4.5 points in the popular vote. How did the pollsters do in forecasting this gap?

Predicting this gap is what most Americans expect from polls. In the Crux Poll, most adults indicated that the purpose of a poll is to know how many points ahead or behind a candidate is. So we will judge the polls on how well they did in forecasting the point spread between the two major candidates.

2. WHICH POLLS SHOULD BE INCLUDED?

Pollsters release hundreds of polls during each presidential election cycle. The number of trial heat polls being conducted increased 900% from 1984 to 2000.[22] With so many polls, we need to decide which ones to include.

Polling organizations sometimes conduct polls without a sponsor. More commonly, polls are paid for by the media, candidates, or private entities such as corporations or political action committees (PACs).

We should not include candidate and PAC polls. They are not conducted with the purest of motives nor fully disclosed (and are challenging to obtain). These polls are often done to drive the news rather than accurately measure public opinion.

Increasingly, corporations are conducting polls to examine the

---

22   Michael W. Traugott, "The Accuracy of the National Pre-election Polls in the 2004 Presidential Election," *Public Opinion Quarterly* 69, no. 5 (2005): 642–54, https://doi.org/10.1093/poq/nfi061.

election's impact on their business and lobbying efforts. Financial institutions, foreign governments, large corporations, and lobbyists of all types conduct polls.

If an election outcome affects a large organization's future, odds are they are conducting polls to predict the victor. They want to steer donations and lobbying efforts appropriately. Corporations know election result can affect their business and their investments. Private polling may explain why the stock market does not move much the day after Election Day.[23] Stock prices reflect the election result before the election is held.

These corporate polls are rarely released, so we cannot include them. They may be the best polls. They are well funded and methodologically sound. The sponsors have no agenda—their goal is knowing what is likely to happen.

Private Corporate Polls are the best

The polls that remain are unsponsored or paid for by the media. These are the polls with the highest awareness levels, the ones the media talk about, and the polls most easy to access. These are what most people think of when they think of "the polls." These are the polls we will assess.

3. WHEN SHOULD THE POLLS BE CONDUCTED?

Poll timing matters. Polls get more accurate as Election Day gets closer. A study by Will Jennings and Christopher Wlezien of more than 26,000 polls across 45 countries and 338 elections concluded:

---

23   Mark DeCambre, "How the Stock Market Performs on, and after, Election Day," MarketWatch, November 9, 2016, https://www.marketwatch.com/story/how-the-stock-market-tends-to-perform-on-and-after-election-day-2016-11-07.

Using polls from 150–200 days before Election Day, the mean absolute error is close to four percentage points; 50 days in advance, it is approximately three points; on the eve of elections, it is under two points. This is not surprising but is satisfying, as it shows that polls become more reflective of the actual result, though they remain imperfect even at the very end of the campaign.[24]

We will use final polls as we assess the performance of pre-election polls. In our analysis, a poll needed to complete its fieldwork no more than two weeks before Election Day and be the last poll the organization published.

Using final polls, which are their most predictive polls, places pollsters in the best possible light. ＼LoL

4. WHICH CRITERIA SHOULD BE USED TO JUDGE POLL ACCURACY?

This is where the analysis gets thorny. There are many ways to decide if a poll is accurate. Pollsters, the media, and academic researchers use different criteria to judge the polls.

What does "accuracy" mean for a poll? Polling accuracy may sound like an easy concept, but it is not so simple on closer reflection. We have chosen to use four criteria to judge polling accuracy.

---

24 Will Jennings and Christopher Wlezien, "Election Polling Errors across Time and Space," *Nature Human Behaviour* 2, no. 4 (2018): 276–83, https://doi.org/10.1038/s41562-018-0315-6.

Criterion A: Was the Poll Better than Random?

One way to judge a poll is to see if it does better than random data. We should insist that polls are better than flipping coins to predict the winner.

Researchers call this a "chimpanzee" choice when nobody is around. Could a group of chimps make this call better than a poll? Polls need to be better than running random data through a survey or a group of excitable mammals pecking at a computer.

A straightforward way to do this is to judge if the poll was better than a 50-50 prediction or a +0 spread between the two major-party candidates. Anyone could guess the two candidates would have the same vote share without taking a poll. This method is free and instantly available!

This might be a capricious standard; it is more challenging to meet in a close election than in a runaway.

We will use it anyway. I can envision a polling editor meeting with a pollster and telling them if they cannot beat flipping a bunch of coins or contracting with a group of monkeys, they will refuse to pay for their project.

We will use this criterion this way. Suppose candidate A wins the election by five points. A random assumption would be that candidate A would receive the same number of votes as candidate B—that candidate A would win by zero points. This arbitrary assumption would have been off by five points.

In this example, a poll "passes" this test if it was within five points of the actual spread, and it "fails" if it forecast a spread of more than five points. The poll needs to come closer to the election result than what would happen by flipping coins.

4b : Page 47

Criterion B: Was the Poll within Its Margin of Error?

Pollsters declare their poll victorious if it predicts within the poll's "margin of error." Focusing on the margin of error is a misguided way to judge poll quality. This leads to confusion. Reporters and pundits (and many researchers) misinterpret the meaning behind the margin of error.

got that wrong on Unit 2
AP Gov test

The margin of error refers to sampling error and is present on every poll or survey. It is calculable. Polls seek to measure what everybody thinks by asking a small group. There is a degree of uncertainty in this.

The formula for the margin of error depends on (1) how many people are surveyed and (2) their response variability. The more people interviewed, the lower (better) the margin of error. The more interviewees give the same response (lower variability), the better the margin of error.

If a poll interviews a lot of people and they all seem to say the same thing, the poll's margin of error is low. If the poll interviews a small number of people and they disagree considerably, the margin of error is high.

Another assumption is used in the calculation for sampling error: the confidence level desired. Nearly every pollster uses a 95% confidence level.

There is no compelling reason to pick this confidence level other than it is what has been historically chosen. Polling methodologists like to have an air of science in their discussions. Yet, they fail to acknowledge they chose this fundamental assumption for their calculations for no apparent reason.

I have never met anyone who knows why researchers chose 95% or why its widespread use continues.[25] Methodologists I asked surmised that 95% was chosen because it "sounds authoritative."

What does it mean to be within the margin of error on a poll? It means the two data points being compared can be deemed different with 95% confidence. Put another way, if we repeated the survey a zillion times, at least 19 out of 20 times (95% of the time), the two numbers would be different. When this happens, there is a significant difference between the two numbers.

In this case, "significant" does not mean "important." It means the two numbers are different.

If Biden leads Trump in a poll by eight points and the margin of error is five points, we are confident he is ahead (his percentage is higher) because this lead is outside the margin of error. Not perfectly sure, but more than 95% confident. The only way to be 100% sure would be to predict Biden will get between 0% and 100% of the vote.

Here is where reporters and pundits confuse matters. Say they are reporting on a poll with a five-point margin of error, and Biden leads Trump by four points. Reporters like to call it a

---

25 There is renewed attention on how arbitrary this choice of 95% is. See Malcolm Ritter, "Sorry, Wrong Number: Statistical Benchmark Comes under Fire," AP, November 17, 2019, https://apnews.com/article/science-us-news-ap-top-news-medication-weekend-reads-12cf3d07354c47b3b9bb552776071522.

"statistical dead heat" or imply the race is tied because this lead is within the margin of error.

Neither is true. The only way to have a statistical dead heat is for the exact number of people to choose each candidate in the poll.

The race is not tied in this example. Instead, there is less than 95% confidence Biden is leading. We might be 90% sure Biden is leading Trump in this example. Why would anyone call that a statistical dead heat?

As polling pioneer Warren Mitofsky once stated:

> If one candidate is ahead of another candidate by a constant number of points over a number of surveys...if there is anybody that would like to bet even money on the second candidate, let me know, I am available for the bet. They are not tied. It is not a dead heat.[26]

Pollsters also misinterpret the concept. They deem their poll "accurate" as long as the election result is within the margin of error. Margin of error accuracy is more of a spectrum than an absolute.

All polls are inaccurate; it is a matter of how inaccurate they are.

Some 2016 final polls were accurate, if accuracy is defined as having the election result be within the poll's margin of error. Since most polls predicted the wrong winner, future textbooks

---

26 "Media Coverage of Presidential Primaries," C-SPAN, January 6, 2000, https://www.c-span.org/video/?154561-1/media-coverage-presidential-primaries&playEvent.

will not present 2016 as exemplary of polling accuracy. The year 2016 is more likely to be taught alongside 1936 and 1948.

Another mistake reporters (and researchers) make is not recognizing that margin of error only refers to sampling error, which is just one of many errors that can occur on a poll.

This book began with a quotation from Humphrey Taylor, the former chairman of the Harris Poll. He states that potential sources of error on a poll are infinite. The poor performance of recent presidential polls has little to do with sampling error and more to do with the types of error Taylor is referencing.

Christopher Adams, Paul Adams, and David Zussman, the authors of a postmortem analysis of a 2017 polling disaster in Calgary, encapsulated this thought well:

> Polls have never been as good as their famous disclaimers imply— plus or minus a specified margin of error, 19 times out of 20. That's because the disclaimer captures only one kind of theoretical statistical error. It does not address, for example, cases where a pollster has written a poor or confusing questionnaire, or sampled the wrong people, or failed to weight the results properly for the characteristics of the population under study.[27]

Sampling error receives far too much emphasis. The calculation of sampling error assumes a probability or random sample, which is never the case in today's polling world. Many errors

---

27   Christopher Adams, Paul Adams, and David Zussman, "Polling and the 2017 Calgary Mayoral Election," *Policy Options Politiques*, August 8, 2018, https://policyoptions.irpp.org/magazines/august-2018/polling-and-the-2017-calgary-mayoral-election/.

in survey research are more relevant to a poll's accuracy than sampling error.

A focus on sampling error exists because it is the most straight-forward error to calculate. The margin of error is helpful to consider but needs to be assessed in the context of all polling errors.

By choosing a 95% confidence level, pollsters admit they will have an election result outside their margin of error once every 20 polls they conduct. If all is well with the polls and 20 polls are reviewed, it is expected that the election result will be outside the margin of error of one of these polls.

meaning 95% confidence is bogus

Our review of recent polls reveals that far more than one in 20 polls have election results outside their margins of error. This fact alone should tell us that polling woes must relate to something beyond sampling error.

Nonetheless, margin of error will be used as a criterion to judge poll accuracy. It is a commonly reported measure, and it would be notable in its absence. The pollsters put it out. They purport that their polls will be accurate 19 out of 20 times within the margin of error they calculate. Let us hold them to that standard.

4c : Page 47

Criterion C: Did the Poll Do Better than Polls Have Done Historically?

Academics favor "mean absolute error" (MAE) when judging poll accuracy. MAE is an average of how far off the polls were. Think of it as the polls' "average miss."

The ideal MAE would be zero. Historically, final US presidential pre-election polls have had an MAE under four points.[28] Polls fielding within two weeks of an election have had an MAE of about two points.

MAE does not consider that polling misses could be in the same direction (because MAE is an "absolute error" measure). Polls should miss equally on both sides of overpredicting and underpredicting a candidate's vote total. Although individual polls all have some degree of *absolute* error, the *total* average error should be close to zero for perfectly executed polls.

MAE should decline from election to election because more polls have been conducted over time, and sample sizes have been getting larger. MAE should be decreasing if the polls are improving. If polls are getting worse, the MAE should be increasing.

An MAE of four points is solid, and pollsters should be proud of this number. A four-point error is outstanding in a survey. I would be a wealthy person if I could assure my clients I could consistently predict advertising effectiveness or new product sales within four points.

Given that a historical MAE for pre-election polls, conducted just before the election, is about two points, using four points is a conservative standard by which to judge them. It should be easy for pollsters to meet.

Staying within the historical MAE is a low bar. There are reasons beyond pollster skill to think polling errors should be

28   Jennings and Wlezien, "Election Polling Errors across Time and Space."

declining. Polling error drops the closer a poll is conducted to the election date.[29]

MAE is what academic researchers use to evaluate polling efficacy. It is likely the best criterion to use when judging a poll's accuracy.

A poll is successful on this criterion if it predicts the spread between the major candidates within four points. We will claim the polls on the whole successful if their average is within four points of the final tally.

A fundamental problem for the 1948 polls was that pollsters did not field any polls in the last month before the election. Today, polls are conducted right up until the day before the election. Today's technologies allow for the fast gathering of data.

Today's technologies, especially online polling, make it possible to conduct polls with large sample sizes, reducing error. There is a clear trend toward more polls being completed and released. This should cause the polls to arc toward accuracy.

For this reason, stating that the polls are as good as they have been historically is not necessarily a compliment—polls should be improving even if pollsters are not.

MAE is a lower hurdle to clear than sampling error. A nationwide pre-election poll with a sampling error of four points would need a sample size of roughly 600 people. Most polls have a sample size of about 1,000, and many survey 2,000.

---

29   Ibid.

By using MAE, we insist the polls get better or that they do not get worse. Everything scientific progresses, so why should the polls be any different? Using an MAE cutoff requires that a poll is better than the long-term historical average of polls.

4d: Page 47

Criterion D: Did the Poll Predict the Winner?

I have had lively discussions with fellow researchers about the purpose of market research studies. Some insist that research provides data and context for a narrative, a "story" told to clients to compel them to action.

I do not see it this way. Although creating a story is nice and often necessary to implement research findings successfully, the story is a means to the actual end: predicting the future.

Market research is business decision insurance. Our clients face a crossroads when they come to us. They might be deciding whether to spend millions to launch a new product. They might be deciding whether to invest in an expensive new advertising campaign. They might be thinking about acquiring a competitor or entering a new country. Market research lowers the risk of these decisions by predicting the future.

We are in the prediction business. George Gallup made his reputation by predicting FDR would win in 1936.

Gallup was further off in his vote prediction in 1936 than almost all the polls reviewed for 2016 and 2020. Gallup's 1936 poll was off by more than the historical mean absolute error of polls, was not better than random, and was not within any reasonable sampling error despite interviewing 50,000 people.

The 1936 Gallup poll failed on three of our four criteria. Who cares? Gallup got his prediction right. He jump-started an industry in the process and remains the pollster Americans most recall 40 years after his death.

Polling accuracy can be judged by whether the pre-election poll predicted the popular vote winner. "Successfully predicting the election outcome" merits inclusion because it drives public and media interest in the polls. We want to know who will win.

The media and public distrust pollsters. This lack of trust does not stem from statistical concepts like margin of error or MAE. Instead, people no longer think polls can be relied on to predict election winners.

WE SHOULD INSIST THAT POLLSTERS ARE BETTER THAN AVERAGE

These are fair criteria to use to judge a poll. Let us say you are a polling editor at a major media outlet. You will spend tens of thousands of dollars on a poll (and hundreds of thousands on your pre-election polling for the cycle).

Your reputation rests on these polls. Get your predictions wrong, and your organization looks silly. Your career may be at risk. Get them right, and you have bragging rights for four years.

It is not too much to ask that your pollster

- does a better job at predicting the election than flipping coins,
- comes within its calculated sampling error,

- is better than the average election pollster has been historically, and
- predicts who will win the popular vote.

Our criteria seem reasonable. Yet, it is unsettling to see how few polls meet them.

DATA USED FOR THIS ANALYSIS

This analysis proceeds in two steps, using different datasets for each. For a historical analysis of pre-election polls (from the 2000 election onward), poll results were sourced from Real Clear Politics (RCP) and the National Council on Public Polls (NCPP). The RCP website was used for elections from 2004 to 2020. We used the final poll from each pollster as long as the poll was fielded within two weeks of Election Day. For 2000, we used the NCPP's poll summary because 2000 polls were not obtainable from RCP.

THE POLLS HAVE NOT BEEN GOOD SINCE 2000

This historical analysis reviewed 95 pre-election polls from the six US presidential elections from 2000 to 2020. Taken in total, here is how the 95 polls performed on the four criteria:

- 54% were better than random.
- 56% were within their margins of error.
- 75% had an MAE lower than the historical average of four points.
- 75% predicted the popular vote winner.

JUST 54% OF POLLS ARE BETTER THAN RANDOM

Beating a random selection proved the most difficult of the four criteria for the polls to meet, especially in close elections. In the last six presidential cycles, pollsters have been only slightly better than running random data through a survey. Much of that success came in 2008.

That bears repeating. If we used a computer program to run random data through the questionnaire, our predictions would have been more accurate than almost half (46%) of the 95 final polls reviewed. Random data would have beaten the average of the polls in four of the six elections, with the exceptions being 2008 and 2016. Random data would have outperformed all the 2000 final polls.

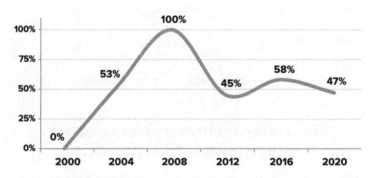

% of Final Pre-Election Polls Performing Better than Random

A LITTLE MORE THAN HALF OF THE POLLS
BEAT THEIR MARGIN OF ERROR

Pollsters focus on the margin of error. All methodologists would concur that 95% of polls should be within their margins of error if conducted with probability samples.

Of the 95 polls studied, 56% were. There is a one in 100,000 chance the difference is due to poor luck and a 99,999 out of 100,000 chance it is not. Something is going on with the polls that is not explained by sampling error as it is traditionally calculated and promulgated.

The ability of polls to come within their margins of error has declined, especially from 2012 onward. Below is the proportion of the polls that came within their margin of error by election year. There is a clear downward trend after 2008.

% of Final Pre-Election Polls that Came within Margin of Error

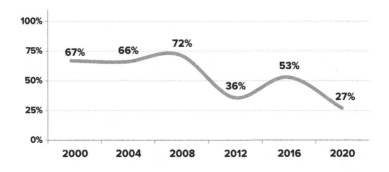

ABOUT THREE-QUARTERS OF POLLS ARE BETTER THAN POLLS HAVE BEEN HISTORICALLY

MAE helps illuminate whether polls are getting better or worse. Polling will always be better in some elections than others, yet the polls should improve as pollsters gain experience and refine techniques.

There has been a clear trend downward in MAE over the past six election cycles, particularly since 2008, which is good news for the pollsters. The polling error is decreasing. Recent polls stack up well compared to polls throughout history.

The chart below shows that from 2000 to 2016, most final pre-election polls did better than the historical error rate. This may have lulled pollsters into a false sense of security. Although there was consternation about the 2016 polls, about three-quarters of pollsters could claim that they beat the historical error rate. In 2020, nearly half of them could claim they were better than the average poll has been historically.

% of Final Pre-Election Polls within Historical Mean Absolute Error

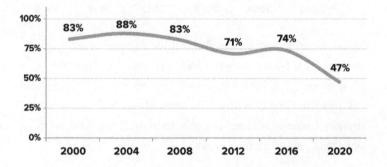

POLLS DO NOT ALWAYS GET THE WINNER RIGHT

The problem is the media and the public do not care about MAE. They simply want to know who will win and by how much. Pre-election polls have done a sporadic job at predicting the popular vote winner. Failure to predict the winner is the source of most bad vibes sent pollsters' way. Pollsters might not like it, but they are judged by getting the winner right.

2012 stands out in this chart. Of the 14 final polls we studied, six had Obama winning, four had Romney winning, and four had the race as a tie. So just 38% correctly predicted an Obama victory.

% of Final Pre-Election Polls Correctly Picking Winner

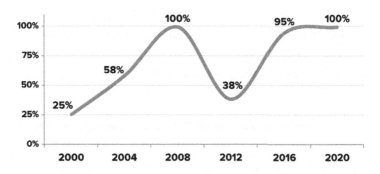

Again, imagine you are a polling editor and you insist that your pollster (1) is better than random, (2) comes within their sampling error, (3) is better than pollsters' historical average, and (4) gets the correct winner. In 2016, about half of the polls I reviewed passed all four criteria. In 2020, I found three final polls that passed all four criteria.

I do not see how anyone doing an honest assessment of recent pre-elections polls could conclude anything other than they have done a poor job.

It is fair to defend recent polls by saying they are a bit more accurate than they have historically been, but this might not matter because the polls have struggled to predict close elections accurately. As elections have become closer, we demand higher accuracy from pollsters, and they are not delivering on our expectations.

Pollsters hold themselves to a different standard than their customers (media, the public, politicians) do. As pollsters, we can claim victory as we watch our field decline in importance because we think we are doing okay.

The answer is not about educating our audiences regarding the limitations of polling and the inherent uncertainty in polling. This is difficult to do, and we have tried to do this and failed. It is simply bad branding for the polling industry to try to convey to the world that we are not as good at what we do as they think we should be.

The answer is to conduct better polls.

ARE POLLING MISSES A US THING?

Polls often fail to perform within their margins of error and are lucky if they are better than random in a close election. The media and public perceptions of them are problematic for pollsters and market researchers.

But is this a US issue? How do America's polls stack up against those in the rest of the world?

I will start with the conclusion: polling miscues are hardly a US-only problem. The day after the 2016 election, FiveThirty-Eight put the 2016 polls in perspective:

> The miss wasn't unprecedented or even, these days, all that unusual. Polls have missed recent elections in the US and abroad by margins at least as big.[30]

---

30 Carl Bialik and Harry Enten, "The Polls Missed Trump. We Asked Pollsters Why," FiveThirtyEight, November 9, 2016, https://fivethirtyeight.com/features/the-polls-missed-trump-we-asked-pollsters-why/.

Market research is conducted worldwide. Sampling methods vary, especially when researching in less developed countries. Pre-election polling takes place in democracies. The pre-election polling field is highly developed in Europe and democracies like Israel, Australia, and Japan. The majority of available data on the performance of polls comes from the United States, Europe, and Canada.

Polling in other countries suffers from similar challenges as polling in the United States. Polling misfires resound in an interconnected world.

It does not take much effort to develop a list of recent polling misses outside the United States:

- **2011: Canadian Federal Election.** Most polls underestimated the Conservative vote. An analysis of the polling flaws for this election[31] implied there was not much wrong with the data pollsters used as inputs. The problems tended to be with what pollsters did with this data when predicting who would turn out to vote (their likely voter models).
- **2012: French Presidential Election Runoff.** Polls tended to show a sizable François Hollande lead during the campaign, yet most final polls predicted a victory for Nicolas Sarkozy. Hollande won by three points. The troubling aspect for pollsters is that few expected a narrow Hollande victory.
- **2013: British Columbia Provincial Elections.** As one news organization put it, "In an unexpected upset that defied virtually every poll, pundit and oracle in British Columbia, the BC Liberals have secured a fourth consecutive majority in

31 Frank Graves, "Accurate Polling Flawed Forecast," EKOS Politics, June 17, 2011, https://www.ekospolitics. com/index.php/2011/06/accurate-polling-flawed-forecast-june-17-2011/.

one of the most stunning electoral victories in provincial history."[32]

- **2014: Scottish Referendum.** Most polls showed those favoring Scottish independence would eke out a victory. The result was a 10-point victory for those favoring remaining in the United Kingdom, well outside the sampling error of any poll taken.

- **2015: UK General Election.** This election involved a serious polling miss, to the extent that FiveThirtyEight issued a mea culpa: "No calculations are necessary to see that we missed badly in our forecast of the UK election."[33] Most pollsters underestimated the number of Conservative seats that would be won.

- **2015: Israel.** Polls showed a tight race and a victory for Isaac Herzog of the Zionist Union party. Instead, Benjamin Netanyahu won a resounding victory, leading CNN to report, "Either Benjamin Netanyahu just staged the most dramatic political comeback in Israeli history and beyond, or something was very wrong with the polls before and during the election."[34]

- **2016: UK Brexit Vote.** Polls indicated the vote would be close, but most predicted that the "remains" would win. Brexit is an example of polling affecting an outcome. Media coverage of the polls resulted in many "remains" staying home because the polls made them confident their side would win.

32 Brian Hutchinson, "Why the Liberals Were Able to Predict Their Victory in BC while Public Election Polls Missed the Mark," National Post, May 18, 2013, https://nationalpost.com/news/politics/why-the-liberals-were-able-to-predict-their-victory-in-b-c-while-public-election-polls-missed-the-mark.

33 Ben Lauderdale, "What We Got Wrong in Our 2015 UK General Election Model," FiveThirtyEight, May 8, 2015, https://fivethirtyeight.com/features/what-we-got-wrong-in-our-2015-uk-general-election-model/.

34 Oren Liebermann, "Why Were the Israeli Election Polls So Wrong?" CNN, March 18, 2015, https://www.cnn.com/2015/03/18/middleeast/israel-election-polls/index.html.

- **2017: Calgary Mayoral Election.** Polls showed the incumbent mayor trailed his challenger by double digits. One oft-cited poll had the incumbent down by 17 points. He won by eight points, making this a 25-point misfire, which may be a record polling miss.[35] Before the election, the pollster with this 25-point error said of the challenger, "Barring some sort of miracle, he'll be the mayor on Oct. 16."[36] This miracle happened.
- **2019: Australia General Election.** The polls overestimated Labour voters. The assessment of the polls for this election in Australia was brutal. The Statistical Society of Australia launched an inquiry into the polls that concluded that what happened was not a polling miss but a "polling failure."[37]

Like in the United States, polling failures in other countries have followed a predictable script: polling misses, subsequent inquiries, and minor tweaks to methodologies deployed in time to start the cycle again for the next election.

Polling mistakes come along regularly and predictably. For decades, these polling misses received little attention. That all changed in 2016, and future polls are likely to meet with a deep level of scrutiny. We have reached another "Dewey Defeats Truman" moment.

35   Christopher Adams, Paul Adams, and David Zussman, *A Review of the Public Opinion Polling Conducted during the 2017 Calgary Election* (Toronto: Marketing Research and Intelligence Association, 2018).

36   Heide Pearson, "Report into Flawed 2017 Calgary Election Poll Results Outlines Several Issues, Offers Recommendations," Global News, August 8, 2018, https://globalnews.ca/news/4375306/report-flawed-calgary-election-polling-mainstreet/.

37   Darren Pennay, Murray Goot, and Phil Hughes, "Inquiry into the Performance of the Opinion Polls at the 2019 Australian Federal Election," Association of Market and Social Research Organisations, October 2020, https://www.researchgate.net/publication/346015338_Inquiry_into_the_Performance_of_the_Opinion_Polls_at_the_2019_Australian_Federal_Election_Report_prepared_by_Polling_Inquiry_Committee.

The polls' performance in 2016 and 2020 has resulted in distrust of pollsters. Let us take a deep dive into how the 2016 and 2020 polls performed.

CHAPTER 3

THE 2016 AND 2020 PRE-ELECTION POLLS PERFORMED POORLY

YOUR VIEWS ON THE PERFORMANCE OF THE POLLS DEPEND ON YOUR PERSPECTIVE

How can we summarize 2016 and 2020 pollster performance? As with most statistical questions, the answer frustratingly begins with the phrase "it depends." It depends on the perspective you choose to take.

- If you ask pollsters, they might say, "Given the challenges of reaching people for polls, the polls get it right. People don't understand that pre-election polls are inherently imprecise and are asking too much of us."
- If you ask an academic researcher, they might say, "The 2016 and 2020 polls were no better or worse than others. We could make the case that the 2016 polls were good because most of them beat the historical errors of presidential polls and that the 2020 polls were average because about half beat the historic average miss."
- If you ask someone in the media or the general public, they might say,

"The polls have been horrible. They failed to tell us Trump was going to win in 2016, and in 2020 they overpredicted Biden's margin of victory."

- If you ask me, I might say, "It is hard not to criticize the 2016 and 2020 polls because so few of them came within their margins of error. There has been a clear deterioration of pre-election poll quality since 2012, and pollsters have not asked the right questions to understand what is going on. I think I will write a book about it."

Each of these statements is accurate, although they contradict each other. Sometimes there is no right and wrong answer to a complex issue, just a difference in perspective.

Polling organizations and academics ignore the media and public perspective at their peril, as there has been a severe loss of confidence in the polls.

This loss of confidence catalyzes a vicious cycle, as pollsters rely on the trust of the people we survey to conduct quality polls. When the public loses faith in the polls, this starts a chain reaction where the data for the next survey suffers, which creates more lack of trust and poorer data for future polls.

This lack of trust launches a cycle that pollsters are struggling to break.

Although pre-election polls performed poorly in 2012, the current consternation stems from the 2016 and 2020 election cycles.

For more detailed analyses of the 2016 and 2020 elections, we used polling databases compiled by FiveThirtyEight.[38] Final polls completed within two weeks of the election were included. Preference was given to polls of likely voters and those using

---

38 Note that because we are switching datasets, some of the results differ slightly from the previous analysis. The conclusions are the same.

a two-candidate horse race.[39] Spanning across the entire campaign, this includes 1,101 polls for the 2016 election and 1,099 polls for the 2020 election.

Twenty-four final polls were released in 2016 within two weeks of the election. Here is how they performed based on the four criteria:

- 67% (16 of 24) were better than random.
- 58% (14 of 24) were within their margins of error.
- 88% (21 of 24) had an MAE better than the historical average of four points.
- 92% (22 of 24) predicted the popular vote winner.

Fourteen of the 24 polls (58%) succeeded on all four criteria in 2016.

Thirty-nine final polls were released in 2020 within two weeks of the election. Here is how they performed based on the four criteria:

- 56% (22 of 39) were better than random.
- 36% (14 of 39) were within their margins of error.
- 51% (20 of 39) had an MAE better than the historical average of four points.
- 100% (39 of 39) predicted the popular vote winner.

Eleven of the 39 polls (28%) succeeded on all four criteria in 2020.

---

39 Specifically, some final polls show results for all respondents, registered voters, and likely voters. When available, likely voter results were used. Similarly, some pollsters include third-party candidates, some do not, and some do both. When there was a choice, we chose the two-candidate race.

2020 was a worse polling year than 2016. The 2020 polls were better than the 2016 polls at predicting the popular vote winner, but that is likely a result of 2016 being a much closer election than 2020. On the critical metrics of coming within the margin of error and MAE, the 2020 pre-election polls underperformed relative to 2016.

The core question is why? Why has a field so reliant on technology performed so poorly in a time of rapid technological progress? Have pollsters figured out what has gone wrong? Are they poised to improve their future work?

CHAPTER 4

POLLING EXPERTS DO NOT HAVE A CLUE WHAT HAPPENED IN 2016 AND 2020

"LATE-BREAKING VOTERS" IS THE GO-TO EXCUSE FOR POLLSTERS

Since the modern polling era began in 1936, when the polls have under-performed, pollsters have explained their mispredictions by stating that something must have happened between the poll and Election Day.

This excuse may have never held water, but it is certainly a stretch for today's polls, which field right up until Election Day with large sample sizes.

It also seems implausible that voters were fickle and changed their minds quickly, especially given the polarizing candidates of the last two elections. It is insulting to imply that people cannot make up their minds about something as important as their next president.

Market researchers set themselves up to use a similar excuse in commercial projects all the time. Suppose a researcher forecasts a new product's sales volume and the client launches the product, and the sales fail to materialize. In that case, to protect themselves, researchers will tend to claim that (1) consumer preferences have changed or (2) the product launched was not the same as the one tested.

In advertising copy testing, it is common for researchers to claim the aired ad differed from the tested one if it performed poorer than predicted. Or that circumstances in the world changed between the time the ad was tested and when it aired.

Highlighting that the world may have changed after the poll is a plausible, standard excuse. It is also the only one we have as researchers when our data is wrong. If our prediction does not hold, either something was wrong with our study, or the world changed in the interim.

We are not apt to blame ourselves, so we blame the world.

THE EXPERTS TRY TO DEFEND THE POLLS

Before discussing likely causes for the recent deterioration of pre-election poll predictiveness, it is interesting to see how pollsters and commentators have responded to the criticism.

The year 2016 was modern polling's *annus horribilis*, although the 2016 polls were more accurate than polls in either the election before (2012) or after (2020). If the media environment in 2016 was as it was in 1948, we would have seen a "Clinton Defeats Trump" headline somewhere.

Because I watched the polls closely, I was shocked and dismayed at the 2016 result. The morning after the 2016 election, I composed a blog post[40] that predicted the polling industry would convene to determine what caused the 2016 miss, that there would be posturing, and that pollsters would make minor tweaks to their methods in time for 2020.

That all happened, yet the 2020 election spurred a similar process. It did not work after 2016, and it is unlikely to work in time for 2024.

AAPOR—POLLING'S TRADE ASSOCIATION

Market researchers and pollsters have excellent trade associations. The American Association for Public Opinion Research (AAPOR) is the most influential when it comes to polling. It is rare to find a reputable pollster that is not an AAPOR member.

AAPOR establishes standards and ethics for polls and pollsters. It conducts studies on the effects of new technological developments (cell phones, the internet, big data, etc.) on polls. AAPOR lobbies for pollsters. They commission task forces and workgroups when problems arise and issue reports. They create educational seminars for researchers. I have enjoyed attending them.

Most importantly, AAPOR is *the* authority that judges poll performance. At least, they are the most referenced authority and the voice of US pollsters.

There are two issues to be aware of when reviewing AAPOR's

---

40   John Geraci, "An Epic Fail: How Can Pollsters Get It So Wrong?" Crux Research, November 9, 2016, https://blog.cruxresearch.com/2016/11/09/an-epic-fail-how-can-pollsters-get-it-so-wrong/.

analyses about pre-election poll performance. The first should be obvious—AAPOR is a trade group of pollsters grading their own work. AAPOR is not independent. Although improving the polls is central to their mission, criticizing the polls is harmful to their membership.

That is not to say AAPOR fails to do a rigorous analysis of polls, because they do—but pollsters are not the most objective judges of their own work. Nobody is.

Having a trade association assess their members' work is like allowing high school students to grade their own tests. Even if they are trustworthy individuals, the incentives are not in the right place.

As a survey researcher, I tell our clients that they should never let their advertising agency conduct research to assess their own work. They should contract with third-party research agencies instead. It is crucial that the party evaluating the work does not have a vested interest in the outcome.

With polls, AAPOR does.

The second concern is that AAPOR has long been influenced by an old guard, a "second wave," of pollsters. AAPOR continues to be influenced not by the pioneers of polling (like Gallup, Roper, Harris, and Crossley) but by firms that spawned from them and pollsters who personally knew these pioneers.

These "second wave" pollsters are incredible. They built today's market research profession and helped make public opinion polls a part of American life. They have tirelessly promoted the need for high-quality polls. I make a living because of a path they blazed. They worked relentlessly to improve the quality of polls.[41]

It would be unfair to say that time has passed AAPOR by, but it *would* be fair to say they are slow to advocate for new developments in the polling world.

AAPOR's conservatism was evident with online polling. AAPOR members (many of whom had significant investments in telephone research centers) resisted online polling. AAPOR's initial reaction to online polling was to outline why it could not work rather than see that it was the inevitable future and work to discover how it *could* work.

Businesses in need of market research began to flock to upstart online research companies in droves. The success of these new companies caused AAPOR and its members to embrace online polling reluctantly.

AAPOR firms were late to the online research party. When they showed up, they claimed they had been there all along and hoped others did not notice.

Although AAPOR represents many, if not most, of the sharpest minds in research and polling, its members have clear incentives to defend the status quo and not be too critical of their work.

---

41 They deserve recognition by name: Andrew Kohut, Warren Mitofsky, Harry O'Neill, and Humphrey Taylor are among the second-wave pioneers.

Nonetheless, many look to AAPOR when judging poll performance.

AAPOR'S 2016 REPORT IMPLIED THAT POLLING'S PROBLEMS ARE SMALL AND FIXABLE

Polling's 2016 issues culminated in the surprising election of Donald Trump. Although most pollsters predicted Hillary Clinton would win the popular vote, few signaled a Trump electoral victory was possible. In their rush to figure out what happened, pundits on both sides of the political spectrum found a convenient scapegoat in the pollsters.

In the wake of 2016, AAPOR commissioned an ad hoc committee of experts from polling firms, the media, and academia. Their resulting publication[42] details what happened in 2016. It begins in a foreboding fashion:

> The 2016 presidential election was a jarring event for polling in the United States. Pre-election polls fueled high-profile predictions that Hillary Clinton's likelihood of winning the presidency was about 90 percent, with estimates ranging from 71 to over 99 percent. When Donald Trump was declared the winner of the presidency in the early hours of November 9th, it came as a shock even to his own pollsters…There was (and continues to be) widespread consensus that the polls failed.[43]

This report is a must-read for anyone interested in assessing the

---

42 Courtney Kennedy et al., "An Evaluation of the 2016 Election Polls in the US," *American Association for Public Opinion Research* 82, no. 1 (2018): 1–33, https://www.aapor.org/Education-Resources/Reports/An-Evaluation-of-2016-Election-Polls-in-the-U-S.aspx.

43 Ibid.

accuracy of polls. Although critical of the 2016 polls, the report has a guarded outlook.

AAPOR's report concludes that in 2016, "national polls were generally correct and accurate by historical standards." This claim is correct in that the average 2016 miss was 1.1 points in our analysis and about 1.3 points in theirs. (AAPOR used a more extensive set of polls than we did, so the datasets are not identical.)

The AAPOR report states (correctly) that the 2016 polls performed near the historical MAE. How can we claim that the 2016 polls were successful when only 58% were within their margin of error, and many predicted the wrong winner?

The AAPOR report acknowledges that 2016 polls underestimated Trump's support in key battleground states in the upper Midwest. Although we did not need an austere committee to tell us that, it is hard to agree with their reasoning why this happened. AAPOR hypothesizes there could have been a change in voter preference between the final polls and the election. This stance implies that the 2016 polls could have been correct after all.

This position ignores the goal of all survey research and polling—to forecast what people will do in the future, not what they will do today.

Pollsters have claimed that the electorate changed its mind between the polling date and the election date every cycle since modern polling began. The electorate is not that fickle.

A good pre-election poll should predict if a respondent will take the time to vote. Predicting the vote is why a pre-election survey is done in the first place. Nobody cares how the electorate would have voted two weeks *before* the election.

In 2016, Clinton and Trump were polarizing candidates. A hypothesis that voters were waffling between them close to the election seems improbable.

People likely made up their minds before final polls were taken—probably much earlier. It is more likely that voters were determining *whether* to vote, but their choice of candidate was likely set.

AAPOR states that many 2016 polls failed to set quotas and weight by education status, which resulted in too many highly educated people in their samples. Improper sampling related to education is accepted as a root cause of the 2016 polling miss and resulted in many pollsters tweaking their 2020 weighting strategies.

This finding caused many 2020 pollsters to create models that would have worked well in 2016 but failed to address new issues that arose in 2020. The 2020 problems stemmed from method-ologists conducting polls as if we were living in 2016.

It is easy to look at past data and find a model that fits what happened. Financial analysts do this all the time, but they are careful to remind us that past performance does not indicate future results.

AAPOR also puts forth that there may have been a "shy Trump voter" effect in 2016. This concept is discussed in more depth later. Shy voters ultimately voted for Trump but did not reveal their preference to pollsters. Interestingly, AAPOR noted this as a possible cause of the polling failure in 2016 when, in 2020, some researchers on the committee authored papers that implied the shy Trump voter did not exist in meaningful numbers.[44]

AAPOR's report suggests clues to a Trump victory were lurking in the polls all along, but the media did not see it and pollsters failed to communicate it effectively. I did an extensive internet search of pollsters' websites and articles in the fall of 2016. I did not find a single quote from a reputable pollster or AAPOR member organization that implied the polling data heralded a Trump victory. I did not find any that mentioned a possibility of a Trump victory.

AAPOR implies that pollsters knew Trump might win and failed to communicate that. A review of their members' press releases shows little doubt in their predictions that Clinton would win.

AAPOR needs to protect its membership. Claiming that 2016 polling challenges stemmed from communication issues is a convenient way to do this.

I have worked in marketing my whole career. I have heard high-level marketers and CEOs say similar things when faced with failure. There are times when I present research data showing their new product is not working out or that their customers

---

44 Scott Keeter, Courtney Kennedy, and Claudia Deane, "Understanding How 2020 Election Polls Performed and What It Might Mean for Other Kinds of Survey Work," Pew Research Center, November 13, 2020, https://www.pewresearch.org/fact-tank/2020/11/13/understanding-how-2020s-election-polls-performed-and-what-it-might-mean-for-other-kinds-of-survey-work/.

are not satisfied. Instead of getting to the root causes of these problems, they sometimes label the problem as a communication issue. As researchers say privately, "Nobody wants to hear their baby is ugly." These clients may have spent years on a new product design, and people may have their careers tied up in it. When the research data implies their idea will not work, they become defensive and blame the marketing department. "The product is fine; we are failing to communicate its benefits."

That is the feeling I had when reading the 2016 AAPOR report. The report remains in the first stage of grief: denial. The 2016 AAPOR report is the pollsters investigating themselves, and these folks have a vested interest to say their product (their research methodology) is sound. Prominent AAPOR members have revenues that reach hundreds of millions annually. The 2016 report has a tone of "it was not so bad; we made small mistakes, but we've corrected them."

That did not work out very well in 2020.

In 2020, the president of AAPOR claimed that the 2016 analysis "dispelled the widespread misinformation that polling in 2016 got it wrong."[45] Two-thirds of 2016 polls were better than random, and only 58% came within their stated margins of error. That is not "misinformation." It is factual, and AAPOR would have been better served to be less defensive and more reflective after 2016.

AAPOR concludes, "A spotty year for election polls is not an

---

45 "AAPOR Convenes Task Force to Formally Examine Polling Performance during 2020 Presidential Election," American Association of Public Opinion Research, February 13, 2020, https://www.aapor.org/Publications-Media/Press-Releases/AAPOR-Convenes-Task-Force-to-Formally-Examine-Poll.aspx.

indictment of all survey research or even all polling."[46] I hope
so, but I am not sure.

THE PEW RESEARCH CENTER IMPLIES THAT
WE EXPECT TOO MUCH OF THE POLLS

The Pew Research Center is a nonpartisan organization that
carries out insightful studies. Part of Pew's mission is to be
"a foundation of facts that enriches the public dialogue." Pew
conducts projects on a range of topics beyond politics, such as
religion, technology, the media, science, and so forth.

Pew has an outstanding reputation within the research community. Their studies are methodologically sound and analyzed
with no discernable bias. I tell fellow researchers that if they
see a study from Pew, they can trust it was done right and had
informed minds behind it.

Because of their credibility, it is interesting to review what Pew
had to say about the 2016 polls.

Pew posted an article on November 9, 2016, one day after the
election. It was as insightful as anything written after more
comprehensive study. I found one section of this article particularly interesting:

> The fact that so many forecasts were off-target was particularly
> notable given the increasingly wide variety of methodologies
> being tested and reported via the mainstream media and other

---

46 Courtney Kennedy, Mark Blumenthal, Scott Clement, and Joshua D. Clinton, "An Evaluation of 2016
Election Polls in the United States," *Public Opinion Quarterly* 82, no. 1 (2017), https://www.researchgate.
net/publication/324499360_An_Evaluation_of_the_2016_Election_Polls_in_the_United_States.

channels. The traditional telephone polls of recent decades are now joined by increasing numbers of high profile, online probability and nonprobability sample surveys, as well as prediction markets, all of which showed similar errors.[47]

Pew implies the causes behind the 2016 miss were likely not from a "mode" effect. The mode used to gather survey data (telephone, online, interactive voice response) and how researchers sampled did not matter. All methods showed "similar errors."

Which begs the question: why was the response of pollsters to the problems of 2016 to refine the way they sampled and their modes of data collection? Why tweak how data were collected if this would not make a difference? Were they fixing the wrong problem?

Later, in 2018, Pew posted a video[48] to their blog to wrap up their thoughts on 2016. This video shows that the 2016 polls accurately predicted the popular vote and implies that the problem was with state-level polling. I agree that 2016 state-level polls did not have the resources or methodological heft behind them they should have had.

Pew indicates state-level polls missed late swings toward Trump in crucial states. Although it is a reasonable hypothesis, little evidence supports this assertion. A late shift in voter behavior can be documented by resurveying respondents after the election, asking them how they voted, and looking for differences

---

47   Andrew Mercer, Claudia Deane, and Kyley McGeeney, "Why 2016 Election Polls Missed Their Mark," Pew Research Center, November 9, 2016, https://www.pewresearch.org/fact-tank/2016/11/09/why-2016-election-polls-missed-their-mark/.

48   Mercer, Deane, and McGeeney, "Why 2016 Election Polls Missed Their Mark."

between how they voted and what they said when polled. Pollsters did not do this because it is expensive.

Assuming state-level polls missed late-breaking voters is conjecture and may not be accurate. Political science research[49] shows that few voters do not make up their minds until the last few days before a major election. The late-breaking vote could still be a causal factor for a poll miss in a close election, but it is unlikely it happened in a widespread fashion.

Either way, blaming late-breaking voters fails to recognize the obvious. The goal of a poll is to predict how someone will vote on Election Day. It is the polls' raison d'être. Predicting how the vote will break late in the process is what pollsters are in the business of doing.

The 2016 state-level polls did not do this. Therefore, they failed.

Perhaps state-level polls failed because of late-breaking Trump voters. But it is the pollster's job to account for this possibility and predict the extent to which it will happen. Nobody hires a pollster to measure who would have won the election a week before Election Day.

Nobody hires me as a researcher to predict today's sales—they hire me to predict what will happen in the future.

Pew asserts that the performance of pre-election polls is not a good barometer to judge whether other polls (opinion polls, market research) are doing a good job. Pew says:

---

49   André Blais, "How Many Voters Change Their Minds in the Month Preceding an Election?" *PS: Political Science & Politics* 37, no. 4 (2004): 801–3, https://www.jstor.org/stable/4488912.

An election poll has an extra hurdle to jump: It not only has to measure public opinion, it also has to predict which of the people interviewed are going to vote and how they will vote—a notoriously difficult task.[50]

With respect for Pew, I have to disagree. I have led thousands of research projects. Pre-election polls are the most straightforward polls I have ever done.

Most market research studies are like pre-election polls in that they seek to predict future behavior. We interview people today to figure out how a broader population behaves tomorrow. Market researchers measure today's attitudes and behaviors to predict what will happen in the future.

Predicting future behavior is particularly hard to do for low-involvement consumer decisions. I have conducted studies on mundane issues. I have done surveys to determine which notebook brand elementary students will buy during the back-to-school season, to find out if the removal of a gram of sugar results in more apple sauce sales, and to see if changing the bottle cap color affects diet soda sales.

These are more challenging issues to research than voter behavior because they involve low-consequence decisions made with little thought on the consumer's part. Opinions are not preformed; they are made on the spot under time pressure during a survey. Having people make up opinions during the survey experience leaves an enormous potential for error.

---

50   Courtney Kennedy, "Can We Still Trust the Polls?" Pew Research Center, May 14, 2018, https://www.pewresearch.org/fact-tank/2018/05/14/can-we-still-trust-polls/.

Research studies for high-involvement and well-considered decisions still have many challenges but are far easier to design. I have conducted studies to predict which college a young person will attend, to determine which vehicle consumers will buy, and to forecast which office technology brands a business manager will buy. These are well-contemplated decisions. As a result, the research is more accurate.

Pre-election polling involves the well-contemplated decisions of voters. The bulk of voters have their minds made up well before Election Day. Minds are made up early in elections with well-known and polarizing candidates.

Think about this: do you know a single person who supported Hillary Clinton but, in the last few days before the election, changed their mind and voted for Donald Trump? That is what experts assessing the 2016 polls would like you to believe happened.

The uniquely challenging aspect of pre-election polling is determining if a person will show up to vote (the "likely voter model" discussed later), not determining for whom they will cast their vote. Predicting turnout is no more difficult than other decisions researchers forecast.

The difference is pre-election polls are held to a high, unachievable standard of precision. My university clients will not fire or ridicule me if I overstate or understate how many applicants will attend a college by a few percentage points. They are more likely to pat me on the back, take me to lunch, and commission another project.

Miss by a few points on a pre-election poll, and you can harm your firm's reputation, and your media clients may mock you on air. They might hand you an abacus.

Although pollsters have much riding on pre-election polls, it is incorrect to assert that polls are particularly challenging studies. Researchers and clients know this, which is why an indictment of the polls is very much an indictment of other types of survey research.

The polls are not all bad, and they are not difficult to conduct. But they need to be close to perfect. The bar is set high.

Pew sums up this blog with an insightful statement: "Yes, we can still trust polls. But it is important to be realistic about the precision they can provide."[51] The core issue is that the "precision they can provide" does not match expectations of what we want the polls to tell us.

The answer for pollsters is not to convince the world that we are not as good as they think we are. It is to get better at what we do.

OTHER EXPERTS FELT THE 2016 POLLING MISS WAS OVERHYPED

Let us look at how others viewed the 2016 polls.

"Experts"—polling insiders and academics—echoed the narrative presented by Pew and AAPOR:

---

51   Ibid.

- The 2016 polls were in line with historical accuracy.
- The problem was with state-level polling.
- Polls make uncertain predictions, so people expect too much from the polls.

The day after the 2016 election, Nate Silver from FiveThirtyEight published an interesting post:

> Given how challenging it is to conduct polls nowadays, however, people shouldn't have been expecting pinpoint accuracy...Our model gave a much better chance to Trump than other forecasts did. But that's not very important. What's important is that Trump was elected president.[52]

Like most pollsters and pundits, Silver claims victory ("our model gave a better chance to Trump than other forecasts did") but at the end concedes this is not the truth about the 2016 polls that matters. What matters is the widespread belief that the 2016 polls blew it and the country ended up with an unexpected president as a result.

That lingers. It is why 2016 will go down in history with 1936 and 1948 as years with polling blunders even though 2016 was a better year for pollsters than 2012 or 2020.

Disparaging pollsters might have been the one unifying feature in our country after 2016. Everybody, regardless of where they fell on the political spectrum, took shots at the polls. On the left, commentators felt pollsters had become incapable of predicting an election result. On the right, commentators saw the 2016 poll

---

52   Nate Silver, "What a Difference 2 Percentage Points Makes," FiveThirtyEight, November 9, 2016, https://fivethirtyeight.com/features/what-a-difference-2-percentage-points-makes/.

performance as further evidence of a "deep state"—a conspiracy that caused pollsters to provide purposeful misinformation to benefit the left.

A few days after the 2016 election, Scott Simon on NPR summarized what most of America was thinking:

> The polls leading up to the 2016 presidential election were wrong, wrong, wrong. Pollsters were wrong. Reporters who cited those polls were wrong on a scale that makes history. But how can that be in a time when there's so many avenues into the minds and hearts of Americans? Aren't polls these days supposed to be scientific?[53]

The media were angry in 2016. Reporters had trusted the polls and based their on-air content on them. They were left looking incompetent. Their reactions were precursors to what they would say on election night in 2020.

WHAT DID EXPERTS SAY ABOUT THE 2020 PRE-ELECTION POLLS?

Fast forward four years to 2020.

It is difficult to overstate the volume of venom that came pollsters' way on election night and afterward in 2020. Frustrations with polling were at a fever pitch. Reactions to the polls' overstatement of Biden's support were swift and severe.

---

53   "Evaluating the State of Polling after the 2016 Presidential Election," *Weekend Edition Saturday*, hosted by Scott Simon, NPR, November 12, 2016, https://www.npr.org/2016/11/12/501819302/evaluating-the-state-of-polling-after-the-2016-presidential-election.

On election night, CNN commentator Van Jones remarked:

> These polls are not to be trusted. There's something wrong with the polling industry because the reason people right now, I think, are hurt is because we got a little bit inflated with these polls.[54]

Jones said this weeks before we could properly analyze the 2020 pre-election polls. Many votes had yet to be tabulated. There was no way of knowing how good or poor the polls had performed when he said this. Votes had yet to be counted in many key states.

Frank Lutz, a well-known Republican pollster, also jumped the gun to bury the polls before many votes were tabulated. One day after the 2020 election, he told Axios, "The political polling profession is done...It is devastating for my industry."[55]

These knee-jerk reactions were understandable but premature. No national media entity had called the race when these statements were made, and senatorial control remained uncertain. Emotions were high. Even the pollsters were self-flagellating. These early concerns turned out to be well founded.

THE 2020 REACTION FROM AAPOR—"WE DON'T KNOW WHAT HAPPENED"

As in 2016, AAPOR convened a task force of experts to study 2020 pre-election poll performance. Most committee members

54 CNN's *Election Night in America*, comment by Van Jones, CNN, November 3, 2020.

55 Jim VandeHei and Mike Allen, "A Safe, Sane Way to Navigate the Vote Count," Axios, November 4, 2020, https://www.axios.com/2020-presidential-election-vote-count-guide-75b8e095-3fa5-40c1-8872-e77e69cdecc6.html.

were different than 2016, which resulted in a more critical tone. The report begins by concisely stating the problem:

> Most national polls accurately estimated that President Joe Biden would get more votes than President Donald Trump nationally, but Biden's certified margin of victory fell short of the average margin in the polls at both the national and state levels. Polling overstated support for Biden relative to Trump, and Biden's 306 –232 victory in the Electoral College was narrower than predicted by many election forecasters.[56]

The AAPOR task force also recognized that the 2020 pre-election polls were poor and reflected a bias toward Biden and away from Trump:

> The 2020 polls featured polling error of an unusual magnitude: It was the highest in 40 years for the national popular vote and the highest in at least 20 years for state-level estimates of the vote in presidential, senatorial, and gubernatorial contests. Among polls conducted in the final two weeks, the average error on the margin in either direction was 4.5 points for national popular vote polls…The polling error was much more likely to favor Biden over Trump.[57]

The 2020 AAPOR task force concluded that polling errors were consistent throughout the polling cycle. Final polls were not any more predictive than earlier polls. This consistency supports an assertion that "late-breaking voters" are not a root cause

---

56 Josh Clinton et al., "Task Force on 2020 Pre-election Polling: An Evaluation of the 2020 General Election Polls," American Association for Public Opinion Research, 2021, https://www.aapor.org/AAPOR_Main/media/MainSiteFiles/AAPOR-Task-Force-on-2020-Pre-Election-Polling_Report-FNL.pdf.

57 Ibid.

of polling woes, as the number of undecided voters declines as Election Day nears. Indeed, as the AAPOR report states, "polling error was not caused by late-deciding voters voting for Republican candidates."

According to our Crux Poll, about 7% of voting Americans indicated they changed *whom they voted for* in the last two weeks before the 2020 election, and about 8% of voting Americans changed their mind on *whether* they would vote.

Of these "changers," 65% voted for Biden, 32% for Trump, and the rest voted for someone else. Of those who decided late, 38% chose not to vote, 32% voted for Biden, 26% voted for Trump, and the rest voted for someone else.

The effect of this fickleness is that Biden netted a 1.0% gain in the last two weeks due to the late-breaking vote. Two things stand out from this. First, not much changed in the two weeks before the election. Voting intentions were stable. And measurable.

Second, it was Biden and not Trump who benefited from momentum in the last two weeks. So it cannot be the case that the polls missed the dynamics that happened late in the campaign.

The Crux Poll does not support a hypothesis that the polls were correct when they were taken, yet a late vote swing favored Trump. The late vote swings went to Biden. Late vote swings made the polls look more accurate, not less accurate.

As in 2016, the 2020 AAPOR assessment shows that a ballyhooed "shy Trump voter effect" is minimal or nonexistent.

AAPOR shows that 2020 polling misses in favor of Democratic candidates were higher in senatorial and gubernatorial races than the presidential race, even within the same state. If there is a shy Trump voter effect, it is likely smaller than shy effects for statewide Republican candidates, who were presumably less polarizing than Trump. Josh Clinton, professor of political science at Vanderbilt University and chair of the 2020 AAPOR task force wrote:

> But in at least one respect, the conclusions of the 2020 task force echoed those of the 2016 task force: We found no evidence that Trump supporters hid their support in the polls when asked who they intended to vote for.[58]

The AAPOR report states there are no clear errors related to data collection mode. Random digit dial phone samples performed as well (or as poorly) as samples gathered online or via other data collection methods. Nonprobability samples performed similarly to methods that purport to provide probability samples.[59]

The AAPOR task force was hesitant to blame likely voter models (LVMs).[60] They show evidence that LVMs were no better or worse at predicting Trump's turnout than Biden's turnout. The year 2020 was a high-turnout election, which, in theory at least, should increase LVMs' accuracy.

---

58 Ibid.

59 A probability sample is when each respondent has a known chance of being selected to take part. A nonprobability sample is when the researcher does not know the chance the respondent would be selected. The difference between the two is important, as most statistical techniques used on polling data require probability samples.

60 Likely voter models are statistical models pollsters use to predict if a voter will vote. They are discussed in depth later.

So if the 2020 polling misses are not a problem in sampling, if people were being honest when answering pollsters' questions, and if the methodologists did an excellent job predicting who would turn out and vote, how could the 2020 polls be flawed?

We are left with the bugaboo of all polls—*nonresponse bias.*

Those who chose to answer polls did not vote in the same way as those who chose *not* to answer them. This bias was most evident among Republican voters—the *types* of Republicans who decided to take part in polls were not as representative of all Republican voters as the *types* of Democrats who chose to take part in polls were of all Democratic voters. As a result, the 2020 pre-election polls came closer to predicting Biden's vote percentage than Trump's.

AAPOR does not come to this conclusion directly or definitively and responsibly states, "It cannot be ruled out that there is a multitude of overlapping explanations for the pattern of polling error." But AAPOR does imply that pollsters learned from the 2016 mistakes in sampling and weighting yet did not expect changes in the nature of nonresponse error.

Pre-election polls ask a simple question about how likely a person is to vote. The AAPOR report suggests that:

> Biden supporters and Trump supporters were equally likely to vote after reporting that they would. Overstatement of the Biden-Trump margin was not a result of Biden supporters saying that they would vote and then failing to do so.[61]

---

61   Clinton et al., "Task Force on 2020 Pre-election Polling."

Methodologists overthink their likely voter prediction models. If trusting people to tell us whether they will vote results in no discernable bias, pollsters should trust the people they survey and stop creating byzantine models.

The 2020 AAPOR report ruled out some potential causes but did not offer many hypotheses for what might have happened. It concludes that the determinates of 2020 polling errors remain unknown.

The 2020 AAPOR report presents a concern for polling's future. To many, participation in polls has become a political event unto itself. This politicization could affect the poll's ability to predict elections

> if Republican-supporting voters have come to believe that polling is "fake news" and a tool of "voter suppression" so that the decision to not participate in a poll becomes a political act. Given the politicization of polling by Republican party leaders, it may be that the people who choose to respond or not differ in their opinions even conditional on observable demographics. This problem would be difficult for pollsters to overcome.[62]

THE 2020 REACTION FROM THE PEW RESEARCH CENTER—PRE-ELECTION POLLING'S PROBLEMS DO NOT AFFECT OTHER TYPES OF SURVEY RESEARCH

The 2020 polls missed in the same direction as 2016. Many recent international polling misses have also understated the support for more conservative candidates. In 2016, many poll-

---

62 Ibid.

sters shook off the apparent bias toward Democratic candidates because a more substantial bias toward Republican candidates occurred in 2012.

In 2016, pollsters passed this off as normal poll fluctuation. In 2020, the Pew Research Center recognized this disturbing trend:

> Looking at final estimates of the outcome of the 2020 US presidential race, 93% of national polls overstated the Democratic candidate's support among voters, while nearly as many (88%) did so in 2016.[63]

About a week after the 2020 election, Pew expressed concern over the pre-election poll performance:

> Many who follow public opinion polls are understandably asking how these outcomes could happen, especially after the fairly aggressive steps the polling community took to understand and address problems that surfaced in 2016. We are asking ourselves the same thing.[64]

Most of Pew's work centers on public opinion,[65] so Pew is less concerned with having an LVM because they try to represent the entire population and not merely those who will turn out and vote.

---

63 Courtney Kennedy, Jesse L. Lopez, Scott Keeter, Arnold Lau, Nick Hatley, and Nick Bertoni, "Confronting 2016 and 2020 Polling Limitations," Pew Research Center, April 8, 2021, https://www.pewresearch.org/methods/2021/04/08/confronting-2016-and-2020-polling-limitations/.

64 Scott Keeter, Courtney Kennedy, and Claudia Deane, "Understanding How 2020 Election Polls Performed and What It Might Mean for Other Kinds of Survey Work," Pew Research Center, November 13, 2020, https://www.pewresearch.org/fact-tank/2020/11/13/understanding-how-2020s-election-polls-performed-and-what-it-might-mean-for-other-kinds-of-survey-work/.

65 Pew stopped doing election horse race polling after 2012.

In that sense, Pew's work is more analogous to market research than election forecasting. Like market researchers, Pew poses many questions on topics and looks for a convergence of opinion before drawing conclusions.

For that reason, it would be suitable for market researchers if poor LVMs caused the problems with pre-election polling. Courtney Kennedy at Pew Research Center recognized this in her 2020 assessment:

> If recent election-polling problems stem from flawed likely-voter models, then non-election polls may be fine. But if the problem is fewer Republicans (or certain types of Republicans) participating in surveys, that could have implications for us and the field more broadly.[66]

Pew's 2020 reaction concentrated on issues with recruitment to their American Trends Panel.[67] Pew has noticed that recently, a segment of Republicans (that happened to be among the most fervent Trump supporters) had become underrepresented in their panel.

So Pew hints at the same conclusion that AAPOR drew—that an issue relating to nonresponse bias is at the core of what went wrong with the 2020 pre-election polls. Pew is working to fix this issue in recruiting and by refreshing its panel membership more frequently.

---

66 Drew DeSilver, "Q&A: After Misses in 2016 and 2020, Does Polling Need to Be Fixed Again? What Our Survey Experts Say," Pew Research Center, April 8, 2021, https://www.pewresearch.org/fact-tank/2021/04/08/qa-after-misses-in-2016-and-2020-does-polling-need-to-be-fixed-again-what-our-survey-experts-say/.

67 Pew's American Trends Panel uses an address-based sample, which is discussed in depth later.

Pew implies that despite the drift in their panel composition, the problem stems more from LVMs than sampling. As a result, market research and opinion polling are not as affected as pre-election polling (because these studies do not use LVMs).

If the root cause of 2020 polling misses lies in nonresponse error, opinion polls would be as affected as pre-election polls. So Pew's conclusion in 2020 serves them well, as placing the blame on LVMs does not call into question the quality of Pew's opinion research.

But it may be in the public's eye. In our Crux Poll, a majority of American adults agreed with this statement: "If pollsters can't predict who will win an election, this means we shouldn't trust them to tell us what America thinks about important issues."

There is a spillover effect of the pre-election polls. When they fail, it causes people to distrust opinion polls as well.

Organizations such as Pew that construct panels need to be careful. Underrepresentation of a specific group in a research sample can be handled if the researcher knows which groups are underrepresented. In 2016, pollsters realized they had underrepresented voters with less education. They tweaked their samples. Yet, the 2020 polls fared worse than the 2016 polls.

This time, pollsters are saying that a subsegment of Republicans was underrepresented in 2020. They are going down the same road of fine-tuning their sampling and expecting a different result in 2024.

Pollsters are making a mistake when adjusting samples in this way because these adjustments are among people whose group membership almost perfectly correlates with voting behavior. We know with near 100% accuracy how "fervent conservatives" will vote.

The reason to increase the representation of "fervent conservatives" on a panel is that they vote overwhelmingly for the Republican candidate. If they voted in the same way as the general population, adjusting the sample would not affect the poll's prediction.

In our Crux Poll, 95% of Democrats indicated they voted for Biden, and 92% of Republicans voted for Trump. As long as we know how many Democrats and Republicans will vote, all we need to do is survey Independents to predict the victor.

By weighting on a characteristic (strength of conservatism/liberalism or political party affiliation) that correlates almost perfectly with what is being predicted (candidate preference), researchers are weighting on what they are trying to predict. They are leading the witness.

This problem arises when researchers try to do too much. Weighting too many characteristics causes findings to become more subjective. The biggest irony in polling is that polling becomes art when data are handed off to the scientists (research methodologists).

Some pollsters claim that polling is both an art and a science. It should not be an art at all. It is the "art" part of polling that causes pollsters to predetermine their poll outcomes rather than allow their data to lead them to a proper conclusion. Their models have become overfit, which means they react more to the noise than the signal in the data.

Why do they do this? The short answer is "because they can." The most elemental issue with the polls is the error caused by nonresponse biases that result from low response rates. Because methodologists cannot fix low response rates, they use the tools they have (sampling and weighting) to wrestle the data into submission. They beat the data up so much that it can no longer speak to them.

This approach worked for a long time. Good statisticians can do amazing things with good data. However, we no longer have good data from polls, and pollsters cannot weight and sample their way out of the box they have found themselves in. Yet, they continue to try.

Relying on methodologists to come to the rescue creates a "garbage in, garbage out" scenario that will not work. Instead, pollsters need to focus on building trust and increasing response rates.

OTHER EXPERTS' REACTIONS TO 2020—IT IS TIME TO WORRY ABOUT POLLING'S FUTURE

In 2020, a group of leading Democratic pollsters, ALG Research, Garin-Hart-Yang Research Group, GBAO Strategies, Global Strategy Group, and Normington Petts, showed moxie by releasing a public statement that admitted their polling failure:

Together, we represent five survey research firms for Democratic political campaigns. During the 2020 election, we worked on the presidential campaign, every major Senate and gubernatorial race, and congressional races across the country...Every one of us thought Democrats would have a better Election Day than they did.[68]

This group of pollsters documented their mistakes and are working to remedy polling's problems in time for 2024. These firms are not generally respected as "objective pollsters"; they are partisan pollsters that use polls to craft and promote messages that favor Democratic candidates.

Nonetheless, the spirit of this group of partisan pollsters is refreshing. They have admitted their polls were not accurate, and although they are competitors, they are banding together to diagnose the problem and apply solutions. We need this spirit from the nonpartisan polling community.

This group's hypotheses on what could have gone wrong in 2020 differ from AAPOR's—they see the problem as either in (1) pollster's ability to predict who will vote or (2) accurately measuring their voter preference.

These hypotheses are as correct as they are basic. A pre-election poll is trying to figure out whom you will vote for and if you will take the time to vote. In a nutshell, 2020 miscalls stemmed from the people answering polls being different from those who did not. This is exacerbated by low response rates to the polls.

The 2020 expert analyses are unsatisfying to read, as they do

---

68 ALG Research, Garin-Hart-Yang Research Group, GBAO Strategies, Global Strategy Group, and Normington Petts, "Revisiting Polling for 2021 and Beyond," Democracy Docket, April 13, 2021, https://www.democracydocket.com/news/revisiting-polling-for-2021-and-beyond/.

not provide clear reasoning for the struggles of the pre-election polls. There is a clear gap in the market: there is strong demand for accurate election predictions, and pollsters are failing to meet this demand.

Fortunately, other ways to predict election outcomes may soon hold sway. Some pollsters are doing it right and provide an example for others to emulate.

CHAPTER 5

MAVERICKS, MODELERS, AND A POLLSTER WHO IS DOING IT RIGHT

A BAD METHOD MAY STILL GIVE AN ACCURATE PREDICTION

Imagine you are in Las Vegas and decide to take your chances at the blackjack table. You feel ready for excitement even though you know the house has an edge.[69] You sit next to me and settle in for the first hand.

You are dealt a 10 and a 2 for a total of 12, and the dealer shows a face card. I am sitting next to you, and I am also dealt a 10 and a 2. Identical hands!

I go first and decide to hit. I am dealt a 7, and I choose to stand at 19.

Now it is your turn. You hit, and like me, you draw a 7. You have 19 and decide to hit. I mutter under my breath. The dealer raises an eyebrow at you as he deals you another card. It is your lucky day, and you draw a 2 and stand at 21.

---

69   A typical house edge in blackjack is about 5%. This means for $100 wagered, your expected return is $95, if you make optimal decisions at every step.

The dealer reveals his hand, and he has another face card for a 20. You win, and I lose.

When we both showed 19 and I decided to stand and you decided to hit, who made the right decision? If you consider only results, you made the right decision because you won and I lost.

But did you make a rational decision at the precise moment when you decided to hit, before you knew what the card was?

The answer is no—the odds were greater that you would beat the dealer with a 19 than you would by taking a card and getting an ace or a 2. Of the 46 cards left in the deck, you had a maximum of six cards (aces and twos not yet dealt) left with which you could win. Your odds of busting were 40 out of 46, or 87%.[70]

I would tell my friends that you are a terrible blackjack player. You would laugh all the way to the bank. Others lurking in the casino would be envious of you and want to talk to you and understand your method. You ascribe your success to your skill, not luck.[71]

There is luck involved with pre-election polling. Every cycle has pollsters who choose nontraditional and risky methods. Some of those polls come closer to predicting the election results than pollsters who seem to make the right decisions all along the way. The winning pollsters are media stars for a time, and they build their commercial research businesses off the attention.

If you stay at the blackjack table long enough with your strategy, you will

---

70 This assumes the dealer is using one deck, which is never the case in casino gambling. Multiple decks are used to make card counting much more difficult.

71 This is known as a self-serving cognitive bias. People tend to overascribe their successes to skill and overascribe failures to bad luck.

eventually lose money. Similarly, some pollsters nail their election predictions, soak up their moment, and fade once they stay at the pre-election polling table too long.

Why? Because their underlying methodology is unsound.

WE ALL WANT TO FIND THE NEXT GEORGE GALLUP

Polling history repeats itself every four years. A lesser-known pollster, deploying nontraditional methods, predicts the US presidential result better than established polling organizations. The media lionizes this upstart pollster. Their success calls into question the integrity of traditional polls.

This phenomenon dates back to the early days of modern polling. For five straight presidential elections (1916 until 1932), the *Literary Digest* called the winner using a discounted, primitive method. Their hot streak was long; today's pollsters with suspect methodologies are exposed much more quickly.

Then, in 1936, George Gallup used new statistical sampling methods to challenge the *Literary Digest* and reveal their unsound practices. It was a remarkable story. A young upstart with a new method brashly challenged the status quo and won the showdown, transforming an entire profession in the process.

There has been an equivalent of a *Literary Digest* in most election cycles over the past generation. Unsound methods can lead to accurate predictions. There has been a proliferation of polls with unsound methods recently.

Unfortunately, there has only been one George Gallup. Polling has never found its "savior"—the person who can develop new methods that make the old methods seem silly. But many false polling prophets have come along.

The media are like Linus waiting for the Great Pumpkin, who never comes. Every cycle, the press discovers a few maverick pollsters who nail their election predictions but, in the end, are exposed and do not become the second coming of George Gallup.

A ROOM FULL OF BROKEN CLOCKS PROBABLY HAS ONE WITH THE CORRECT TIME

Just as poor decision makers sometimes cash in at the blackjack table, these maverick pollsters are probably getting lucky. As AAPOR points out in their 2020 report:

> Individual polls may have low error for arbitrary reasons and their current good performance may not necessarily indicate future success…Procedures that are not grounded in statistical theory or theories about the data generating process may employ arbitrary adjustments. Such procedures may produce seemingly "accurate" results that fail to generalize to other elections.[72]

The story goes like this: A renegade pollster using what is called by purists "a questionable method" performs better than the polling establishment. The polling establishment pushes back. The media embraces the maverick because it is a compelling story.

---

72 Clinton et al., "Task Force on 2020 Pre-election Polling."

It is a story we want to hear. Outlier polls are more newsworthy and exciting than polls that say what everyone already knows.

The maverick pollsters' unsound methods result in an inevitable fall from grace. The maverick hits on 19 and is dealt a 2. They cannot replicate this success long.

I am reminded of an event I attended about 20 years ago. The keynote speaker was a trend forecaster who was on television a lot and had written some bestselling books. She ran through her top 12 trends for the upcoming year.

One of them was that "smell will become an important internet feature." Yes, she predicted that technology would permit scent devices to be placed on computers. Website owners could control them (presumably through some Smell-O-Vision wizardry) to extend our interactive experiences to another sense.

A year later, I saw her on a morning show where the hosts praised her because one of her predictions came through (she had predicted that touch-screen technology would come to smartphones). Yet, the hosts did not ask her about the insanity of her prediction that smell would become part of the digital world. She made a dozen bold predictions, one in 12 came true, and she built a reputation based on it.

The "maverick" pollsters tend to do a similar thing. They make bold predictions, occasionally one of them comes true, and reporters and readers overlook the wrong predictions pollsters made.

Pollsters conducted more than a thousand polls in the 2020

election cycle. With that many polls, there will (predictably) be a few that accurately forecast the vote. While a broken clock is correct twice a day, if you walk through a room with hundreds of broken clocks, odds are, one of them is correct *right now*.

Someone is going to nail it.

Most pollsters should nail it—the laws of statistics would suggest predictions should coalesce around a number. That number should be the election result unless there is something fundamentally wrong or biased in how pollsters conduct polls.

We expect a spread in pollsters' predictions. Observers should get nervous during election season if all the polls have the same forecast, as this is evidence of a problem called herding.[73] If the same pollster did the same poll hundreds of times, results would vary predictably. Lurking in the spread of polls will be a few that nail the election result. This is a concept taught in any introductory statistics course.

Another analogy may help. Take 100 coins. With a magic marker, number them from one to 100. Place them in a bag and shake them up. Flip these coins daily for the next month. Record which ones come up heads and which ones come up tails. Look at the stock market performance each day and record if the market went up or down.

It will likely be the case that one coin predicted stock market returns by landing on heads on the days the market was up and landing on tails on the days the market was down. Say that coin

---

73 Herding refers to suppressing polls that seem to stray from what other polls are finding. This is detailed later in this book.

#44 came close to predicting the market's movement. All you have to do to predict tomorrow's stock market performance is flip coin #44, right?

This example illustrates why correlation and causation are two different concepts. The more coins you use in this example, the better the chance one will match the stock market's performance.

If enough pollsters do enough polls, chances are high a few will be predictive. Success in one election cycle could mean the pollster knows what they are doing, or it could imply they were lucky. Their coin came up.

The flaws of traditional pollsters and the current partisan media environment have created a gap where these mavericks with unsound methods thrive. There are so many pollsters out there that you can find one who confirms your view of the world if you search hard enough.

ARE POLLSTERS SMARTER THAN A FIFTH GRADER?

Here is an extreme example of a maverick poll. What if I told you a poll was conducted each presidential cycle from 1956 to 2008 and predicted the presidential winner all but one time?[74] You might be apt to think this poll must be onto something, as it predicted 13 of 14 elections correctly.

What if I told you that K–12 teachers conducted this poll by staging mock elections with their students (not yet of voting age)

---

74   Maria Glod, "As Kids Go, So Goes the Nation," *The Washington Post*, November 3, 2008, https://www. washingtonpost.com/wp-dyn/content/article/2008/11/02/AR2008110201883.html.

weeks before the election and reported results to a nationwide company without a pollster on staff? Would you still trust it?

I have described the *Weekly Reader Student Election Poll*, which shows it is possible to get lucky multiple times with polls with no defensible methodology. The *Weekly Reader Student Election Poll* received widespread media coverage. It is an exemplar of incredible corporate public relations but not incredible polling.

The *Weekly Reader Poll* highlights that not only past performance should establish a poll's credibility. A trusted poll should have a methodology that makes intuitive sense and follows the laws of statistics. Polls should only garner attention when they adhere to accepted standards.

THE RISE OF THE 2020 MAVERICK POLLSTERS

Several "maverick" pollsters came to prominence in 2020 because their predictions presented a counternarrative to traditional pollsters, most of whom predicted that Joe Biden would defeat Trump by eight to ten points.

The media fawned over these maverick pollsters because they set the stage for a story that traditional pollsters might be wrong. The narrative was that the pollsters missed horribly in 2016, and these mavericks predicted they would miss again.

This storyline harkened to 1936, when George Gallup publicly challenged the *Literary Digest*. Gallup purposefully created a stir and became a media star. Gallup was the Joe Namath of polling—guaranteeing what seemed like an unlikely victory and then pulling it off.

The difference is that in 1936, George Gallup had a superior method. That may or may not be the case with today's maverick pollsters.

In 2020, some pollsters became favorites of conservative media outlets and former President Trump's Twitter account. A mistrust of pollsters (on all sides, not just the right) paved the way for these pollsters, who stood out by being different than others, to flourish.

Further, the mavericks' final polls seemed accurate on election night 2020, before all votes were counted. These polls received considerable media attention on election night and for a few days following.

When vote tallies drifted toward Biden during the week or so that followed, the story's arc had ended. News outlets failed to go back and note that these final polls were off as much as everyone else's, albeit in a different direction.

The mavericks also picked the wrong 2020 winner with an error about the size of the average 2016 polling miss but were not called to task as the 2016 pollsters were.

It is a story we yearn to hear. We feel that pollsters are not good at predicting elections, and we want to find the next polling wizard. We need the next George Gallup.

Instead, we might be finding the broken clock that happens to show the current time.

These pollsters have ideological biases they do not attempt to hide. These biases are in a conservative direction. As we will demonstrate later, methodological issues with sampling have caused poll results to drift in favor of more liberal candidates over the last 10 years. What seems to be happening is the conservative bias of these maverick pollsters is compensating for this drift.

The challenge is to understand the causes of this drift to the left and fix it. Adding in a compensating bias is not a solution. Two wrongs in opposite directions do not make a right.

All that said, establishment pollsters need to realize that these maverick pollsters are having success and gaining trust at a time when that is sorely needed.

The maverick pollsters are doing some intelligent things by experimenting with new approaches. For instance, they use larger sample sizes, a mix of data gathering methods, and concentrate their polling resources on swing states.

What I appreciate most about these pollsters is they show empathy for their respondents in a way that traditional pollsters do not. They keep their questionnaires short and easy to answer. They do all they can to keep the burden on poll-takers low.

They also experiment with different ways to ask the key question in a pre-election poll: *Who will you vote for?* They have posed questions about who people think their neighbors will vote for, who they think will win, and who they would put their money on if they had to wager on the election. These approaches are not new, but they may work in elections with highly polarizing candidates.

The mavericks are also more forward-looking than establishment pollsters. Establishment pollsters are obsessed with modeling data to past elections, while the mavericks take a hard look at the current environment and adjust their methods accordingly.

These are helpful experiments. However, these mavericks are not forthcoming with the details of how they are collecting data and how they are asking questions. They revel in running afoul of the rules of disclosure established by polling trade groups.

This causes them to run afoul of the polling establishment. And their overt partisan biases cause most traditional pollsters to bristle. Because of their antagonistic reaction to the mavericks, traditional pollsters are not receptive to learning from the elements of their polling operations that are working.

Although these maverick pollsters have had some success, they seem to be no more or less successful than other pollsters. They have missed many election calls yet have convinced the media they are the next George Gallup.

Are they onto something? It will be hard to tell until they disclose their methods and put what they are doing up for scrutiny.

DO "SHY" RESPONDENTS EXIST?

Conservative maverick pollsters play off a notion of a "shy" respondent. This concept is a belief that a large proportion of Trump voters are uncomfortable telling a live interviewer they intend to vote for Trump, so they lie. A shy effect, if more present among conservatives than liberals, results in polls overstating the liberal candidate's vote percentage.

Credible research organizations have studied the shy voter phenomenon. The Pew Research Center has concluded that their research "has failed to turn up much evidence for this idea."[75] There is little indication shy Trump respondents existed in significant numbers in either 2016 or 2020.

Shy Trump respondents may exist, but if they do, it is not happening enough to matter to the forecasts.

The notion of a shy (i.e., dishonest) respondent is not new. The concept was extensively discussed during the Kennedy campaign in 1960 and the Reagan campaign in 1980. Supporters claimed that a shy Kennedy voter was afraid to express their support because Kennedy was Catholic. Later, a shy Reagan voter was surmised because of Reagan's conservative views. Both candidates ended up doing better than the polls suggested they would.

There is limited academic support for these assertions, which the campaigns created to buffet the poll numbers and make their candidates look viable. The shy effect was more of a campaign tactic than an actual problem for the polls.

The shy voter effect is sometimes called the Bradley effect. In 1982, the polls overestimated support for Tom Bradley, a Black Democratic candidate for the mayor of Los Angeles. The theory was that white poll takers would tell pollsters they supported a Black candidate because that was socially acceptable. But on

---

75   Courtney Kennedy, Scott Keeter, Andrew Mercer, Nick Hatley, Nick Bertoni, and Arnold Lau, "Are Telephone Polls Understating Support for Trump?" Pew Research Center, March 31, 2017, https://www. pewresearch.org/methods/2017/03/31/are-telephone-polls-understating-support-for-trump/.

Election Day, these voters cast their vote for his opposition, the white candidate.

The Bradley effect is problematic because if it is believed, it can curtail the fundraising ability of minority candidates and thus limit the ability of minorities to win elections. Academics are mixed in their views on whether it exists. Most feel this issue has diminished over time and that the election of Barack Obama proved the Bradley effect is no longer present. The polls *underpredicted* Obama's support in 2012.

We covered the shy voter concept in the Crux Poll. Eight percent of American adults indicated they have lied on a survey or a poll. Half (50%) of those who admit to lying voted for Biden, 30% voted for Trump, and the rest voted for someone else or did not vote.

In the Crux Poll, if there was a shy effect, it was small and benefited Biden and not Trump. (Of course, this assumes those who took the Crux Poll told the truth about lying!)

The same poll showed that 65% of Americans feel that *other people* lie on surveys or polls. The belief that there are dishonest respondents has taken hold. We tend to believe that shy respondents exist, even if they do not.

FiveThirtyEight[76] documented that in 2016, Trump was more likely to do better than the polls predicted in red (Republican-leaning) states than in blue (Democrat-leaning) states. This pattern is the opposite of what would be expected if shy Trump

---

76 Harry Enten, "'Shy' Voters Probably Aren't Why the Polls Missed Trump," FiveThirtyEight, November 16, 2016, https://fivethirtyeight.com/features/shy-voters-probably-arent-why-the-polls-missed-trump/.

voters existed. FiveThirtyEight points out that Republican Senate candidates also outperformed the polls, implying that whatever happened was not specific to Trump.

So although the maverick pollsters build their case on the shy voter effect, the evidence for it is thin. It seems more likely that those who do not wish to show their support for a candidate will refuse to participate in the poll rather than participate and lie.

The worry for traditional pollsters is that this may become a self-fulfilling prophecy—the considerable talk about people lying on polls could cause it to happen. Although it seems unlikely that people are lying to pollsters, it could happen in the future.

PEOPLE DO NOT LIE, BUT THEY MAY TELL POLLSTERS WHAT THEY WANT TO HEAR

A similar bias is known as a "social desirability bias." This type of error is more subtle than claiming people lie to pollsters. It is well known that the presence of an interviewer can influence answers to sensitive questions.

I lead many polls that relate to youth and risk behaviors. Public health researchers have established that adolescent drug and tobacco use is underreported on surveys. The underreporting depends on the method. Methods that involve a live interviewer find the least teenage drug use. Surveys proctored by authority figures (teachers, parents) underrepresent drug use. The methods that come the closest to actual results are mail and online surveys, which are self-administered.

This mode effect influences sensitive questions in the other direction as well. Telephone surveys (with an interviewer present) find people go to church, believe in God, and donate to charities at higher rates than do online surveys (with no interviewer present).

Social desirability bias refers to a tendency for a person to want to give a socially acceptable answer in a social situation, such as when an interviewer is posing questions. It is subtle and unintentional—people want to answer in an expected and accepted fashion. People want to be nice.

This bias may exist in the 2020 telephone surveys to the degree that saying you will vote for Trump is not a socially desirable response. But it is unlikely that a social desirability bias away from Trump existed in 2020, as all modes of data collection got similar results for his vote percentage. Online and live-caller polls get identical results, which suggests that current social desirability biases in pre-election polls are small.

In 2016, a social desirability bias existed on both sides. It was not popular to tell others you supported either Trump or Clinton. According to Gallup:

> Donald Trump and Hillary Clinton head[ed] into the final hours of the 2016 presidential campaign with the worst election-eve images of any major-party presidential candidates Gallup has measured back to 1956.[77]

I could not do what I do for a living if I sincerely felt that people lie on surveys. Do people provide inaccurate information?

77   Lydia Saad, "'Trump and Clinton Finish with Historically Poor Images," Gallup, November 8, 2016, https://news.gallup.com/poll/197231/trump-clinton-finish-historically-poor-images.aspx.

Absolutely. But this is likely more of a consequence of poorly designed questionnaires, fatigue, or a lack of engagement with the survey topic than a respondent's willful intent to mislead.

The people we survey have no apparent reason to lie when responding to a poll. According to Anthony Salvanto of CBS News:

> No one needs to be in a poll in the first place. It's not clear why someone would invest the time and energy of taking a poll at all, just to spend their time lying their way through it. It's more likely they would outright refuse to take the poll.[78]

Salvanto is correct—there is no incentive to lie on a poll. The issue for pollsters is about a response bias. Does the tiny fraction of those who lie about who they will vote for skew to one candidate or another?

Pollsters should be worried that two out of three American adults think others lie on surveys and polls. This can become a self-fulfilling prophecy. Few people currently lie on polls. But if participating in polls is seen as a political act unto itself, this could become an issue in the future.

NERDS RULE! THE ELECTION FORECAST MODELS

Popular vote predictions have traditionally been made from polling data. A new approach has emerged that involves sophisticated statistical models.

---

78 Anthony Salvanto, *Where Did You Get This Number? A Pollster's Guide to Making Sense of the World* (New York: Simon & Schuster, 2019).

These models use many polls as inputs. The better ones balance these polls by past pollster performance. Although poll results are the most critical input, other factors are considered. These models consider political party registration, approval ratings, demographics, fundraising, measures of partisanship, and so on.

But polls are their crucial input. These models live or die with the quality of the polling data they use.

FiveThirtyEight is the best-known firm that uses this approach. FiveThirtyEight does not conduct polls. FiveThirtyEight is a media organization (currently owned by ABC News) that contains articles, blog postings, podcasts, and so forth, built on its predictive modeling capabilities. FiveThirtyEight predicts the probability of events happening in the future using advanced techniques. It pioneered a new method of forecasting election results—and an approach to news called data journalism.

In the 2020 cycle, *The New York Times*, *The Economist*, and Lean Tossup all had similar models. These organizations use these models to run simulations. The output is the probability of each candidate winning.

This modeling is interesting to people who have a statistical background. It is likely confusing to those who do not.

Pollsters feel organizations that construct these models have unfairly built their businesses by intercepting their work. Pollsters bristle at the mention of FiveThirtyEight because FiveThirtyEight doles out grades to pollsters.[79] Nobody likes an outside organization critiquing their work.

---

79 "FiveThirtyEight's Pollster Ratings," FiveThirtyEight, March 25, 2021, https://projects.fivethirtyeight.com/pollster-ratings/.

Poor FiveThirtyEight grades have led to clients firing pollsters. Who wants to work with a pollster that has a grade of C when you can hire an A?

Does it make sense to compile polls into averages? Can this work? Does it result in better predictions?[80]

The short answer is yes. Compiling and averaging polls allows researchers to increase the certainty around a prediction. Compiling polls does not have the same statistical benefits as larger sample sizes, but it is close.

There are caveats. First, it makes no sense to include poor-quality polls in an average, even if these polls are weighted downward. Poll aggregators should only compile polls that meet an industry standard for quality and disclosure. Including bad polls creates a "garbage in, garbage out" scenario.

These modelers take an objective, scientific approach. But by considering so many polls, they legitimize the bad ones. Only polls with similar methods should be compiled, and it is unclear if these modelers are doing anything to vet the quality of polls they use as inputs.

The more consequential problem with aggregating polls is if there is a fundamental bias[81] in how the pollsters are doing something, compiling polls will not solve this. Aggregation can magnify the bias. An issue pollsters had in 2016 and 2020 was

---

80 The law of large numbers would imply that the more polls analyzed, the closer the average of them should be to the true measure of what the electorate thinks.

81 We are using the term "bias" in its statistical definition. We mean a systematic drift in the distribution of the data.

that, with few exceptions, they did not miss the result by much, but they all were off in the same direction.

I admire the predictive modeling approach. Rather than discuss point differences and sampling errors, these models yield what many want to know: what is the chance of my candidate winning the election? Probabilities are a better way to forecast because they connote uncertainty and that no prediction is perfect.

In the Crux Poll, Americans were split on what the goal of a poll should be. Fifty-four percent felt it is better to know how many points ahead or behind a candidate is. Forty-six percent thought it is better to know a candidate's probability of victory.

Four criticisms of the predictive modeling approaches have merit.

First, probabilistic predictions are, by their nature, never technically wrong. The probability of a candidate winning will never be 0% or 100% until the election is certified.

This ambiguity gives these modelers plausible deniability when something is wrong within their model. In 2016, FiveThirtyEight's model gave Trump a 29% chance of winning. After the election, they could claim "we told you he had a chance" rather than what most readers interpreted from their forecast, which was "he is not going to win."

As it happened, FiveThirtyEight declared victory by communicating that although they favored Clinton, their models gave Trump a greater chance than others. That is like saying I am a better blackjack player than you because I hit on 18, and you hit on 19.

Second, these modelers blame polling inputs when the improbable happens in an election. If there is a systematic problem with the polls during an election cycle, the models will reflect that. Polls are the primary inputs for these models.

The modelers will claim that the polls had biases in their sampling, that they did not account for late voting swings, or that the state-level polls were of poor quality.

Academic researchers will tell you that you are responsible for the inputs you choose to use in your model. These modelers do not embrace this responsibility.

It does not sit well with me when the modeling firms criticize the polls. These modelers intercept the work of pollsters without compensating them or even showing appreciation. It is sort of like complaining about the free beer a bartender gave you that you did not even thank him for. If you do not like it, pay for your own beer, or in the modeler's case, do your own poll!

Third, these modelers include almost any poll with a modicum of credibility. These modeling firms are loose in which polls they will include as inputs. They include polls of suspect quality, polls done by organizations that prioritize driving the news agenda over measuring public opinion, and those with a poor record of predicting elections. More data is not always better.

FiveThirtyEight has an objective process for grading pollsters.[82]

---

82   Nate Silver, "How FiveThirtyEight Calculates Pollster Ratings," FiveThirtyEight, September 25, 2014, https://fivethirtyeight.com/features/how-fivethirtyeight-calculates-pollster-ratings/.

Their model would be better served by removing all polls from pollsters below a particular grade level. Although they weight polls from poor-performing pollsters downward, their models would be better if they excluded them—garbage in, garbage out.

Finally, these models suffer from a "black box" problem. Despite pollsters' attempts to explain their model, few reporters who use their predictions understand them. I have not met anyone from the polling world who has more than a conceptual understanding of these models.

Pollsters who provide the inputs for these models are pressured to be transparent in their methods. The modelers should be held to that same standard.

Whether these models result in more accurate predictions than a carefully conducted poll is unclear. The general concept is sound. More information (i.e., more polls) should make for a better forecast. Model makers face a challenge in educating the public and their media clients on probability. That is no easy task.

Although the various modelers use similar approaches, their models are not all the same. As data-driven as they are, these individuals must make subjective choices along the way. They partially rely on the "art" or the "gut feel" of experts. Because these models all have access to the same polls as inputs and do not always come to the same predictions, there must be subjectivity in the process.

For these firms, the stakes are high, and reputations are on the line. This has led to public feuds and Twitter wars among modelers.[83]

Compiling polls into a polling average and considering information beyond the polls to make election predictions is an excellent idea. Media organizations should report polling averages and modeling probabilities instead of the findings of any specific survey.

This requires that journalists understand the subtleties of the numbers. Pollsters need to embrace this responsibility. As a researcher, my job is not to provide good data to my clients; it is to be sure that they understand this data and make better decisions based on the studies they do with me. The pollster's job is not to provide good data; it is to be sure that journalists use this data to tell accurate stories. Major media companies do not need unique polls; they need unique insights from the polls.

WHO IS DOING IT WELL?
POLLING ASSOCIATED WITH COLLEGE POLLING CENTERS

There are colleges and universities that maintain polling centers. These are exciting entities from the colleges' standpoint. These polling centers support an academic mission while building the school's brand presence.

College polling centers do not tend to be at leading research institutions or selective schools with nationally established brands. With exceptions, these polling centers are at regional

---

83   Matthew Zeitlin, "'Nerd Wars: Nate Silver and G. Elliott Morris Are Trying to Make Sense of the 2020 Election—and Each Other,'" *The New Yorker*, October 15, 2020, https://nymag.com/intelligencer/2020/10/nate-silver-and-g-elliott-morris-are-fighting-on-twitter.html.

private colleges. Many of these colleges would not be known outside their local markets if not for their polling centers.

Establishing a polling center can benefit a college's brand as much as getting a team into the NCAA basketball tournament, at considerably less cost and risk. Had anyone outside their local markets heard of Gonzaga or Xavier before their college basketball success? Similarly, Quinnipiac, Marist, and others would not be nationally known if not for their polling centers.

College polling centers do much more than enhance a college's brand. They provide student employment. They give students real-world experience in research and polling, thus making them more desirable job candidates. They provide data professors can use in their research.

The polling centers likely provide revenue to the colleges, as these centers use low-cost labor (students) and can tap into existing computing resources at the college at a low cost. A study gains credibility when the name of a college or university is attached to it.

Moreover, pre-election polls that come from college polling centers are excellent. You can make a case that they are more accurate than polls conducted by the most famous polling brands.

The public thinks so. In the Crux Poll, 57% of Americans trusted polls from colleges more than they trusted polls from polling organizations.

Here are the FiveThirtyEight pollster grades for the better-known college polling centers:[84]

- Sienna College: A
- Monmouth University: A
- Marist College: A
- Emerson College: A–
- Quinnipiac University: A–

These are fantastic grades, and FiveThirtyEight are tough graders. Here are their grades for the five best-known polling brands:[85]

- Survey Monkey: C
- Gallup: B+
- YouGov: B+
- Ipsos: B–
- Pew: B–
- Harris Insights & Analytics: B+

The college pollsters are the A students, and the traditional pollsters are the B students.

College polling centers measure up nicely compared to polling firms. But why? After all, polling firms are stacked with professionals who have been polling for decades and have worked on hundreds of polls. Most college polling centers are staffed by students, with a professor or two overseeing the process. This

---

84   As of January 1, 2022.

85   These were the five polling brands with the highest awareness levels in the Crux Poll.

professor likely has polling experience but also teaches, supervises graduate students, publishes research, and more.

Polling is not the sole expertise of the people overseeing these centers. Polling is not a university's core competence. Yet, these centers do a fantastic job.

Why?

One reason is that their primary mission is academic, and they are not profit-oriented. These college centers exist to teach students about the polling field and garner attention for the university in the process.

Since their employee base is not filled with workers who have been doing polls for decades or methodologists working with poll data full time, college polling centers will likely keep it simple. College polling centers do not tend to overcomplicate. Many polling firms do.

College polling centers are run by well-respected individuals. These leaders do not face the same challenges as the CEOs of polling firms, who are under pressure to grow their firms and turn a profit for their investors.

College polling centers conduct a small volume of work compared to polling firms. Their leaders are hands-on in a way senior-level people at polling firms are not. Most college polling centers concentrate on opinion and pre-election polls. Polling firms do all types of studies.

Polling firms relegate their pre-election and opinion polls to a small team of researchers. Polls are a tolerated financial nuisance in a for-profit firm. Opinion polls are likely less than 5% of the total revenue of most polling firms.

College polling centers have solid and well-respected brands. People trust colleges much more than pollsters. Respondents are likely more apt to cooperate with their surveys.

The college polls do not suffer from the public's perception that they are "biased" like the polling firms sometimes do. In our Crux Poll, colleges and universities were trusted by over twice as many Americans as pollsters were.

College polling centers are transparent in their methods and findings. They do not have trade secrets to protect. By the very nature of universities, when they discover that something works, they publish it to share with the world. It is part of a college's mission to move a knowledge base forward.

Although it is difficult to tell for sure, I suspect college polling centers suffer far less from "herding" than polling firms, as it is less risky for them to put out a poll that does not conform to expectations. The result is, they have been more accurate than the polling firms.

THE DES MOINES REGISTER AND SELZER & CO. HAS FIGURED SOMETHING OUT

Let us look at a pollster that is doing something right. J. Ann Selzer is the president of Selzer & Company and conducts the Iowa Poll for *The Des Moines Register*. All eyes are on her during pivotal moments in the election cycle because of the importance of Iowa caucuses to the presidential election. I have seen a cable network have a countdown timer letting people know the minutes and the seconds left before the Iowa Poll will be released.

Selzer has a FiveThirtyEight pollster grade of A+.[86] Four pollsters currently receive this A+ rating.[87] FiveThirtyEight declared Selzer "the best pollster in politics"[88] in 2016.

Selzer has been conducting polls since 1994. She first came to national prominence in 2008 by predicting Barack Obama's resounding victory in the Iowa caucuses when no other pollster did. Her track record is enviable—Selzer has closely forecast vote margins in the caucuses, senatorial races, and the general election in Iowa. You would be hard-pressed to find a race she miscalled.

Selzer's final 2020 poll had Donald Trump beating Joe Biden 48% to 41% in the state of Iowa. This was news. The media declared the poll an outlier, as most other polls in Iowa projected the race as a toss-up or a narrow Biden victory. The media questioned whether Selzer's winning streak had come to an end.

In the end, Trump won by 8% in Iowa. The Selzer poll was the only one to predict a resounding Trump victory.

Selzer is not a case of a lucky, rogue pollster that got it right. This polling is based on sound methodology that resists the

---

86 As of January 1, 2022.

87 As of January 1, 2022, the pollsters receiving an A+ rating from FiveThirtyEight were Selzer & Company, ABC News/*The Washington Post*, Sienna College/*The New York Times* The Upshot, and IBD/TIPP.

88 Clare Malone, "Ann Selzer Is the Best Pollster in Politics," FiveThirtyEight, January 27, 2016, https://fivethirtyeight.com/features/selzer/.

temptation to overcomplicate a simple form of market research. Selzer does not prevail against conventional wisdom. Instead, she returns to what made polls work in the first place.

It is helpful to look at what Selzer is doing right. Her methodology stands out for how old school and boring it is.

She is doing what the best polls from a generation ago did. Her polls are telephone based. She is careful not to recontact previously surveyed people. She draws samples carefully and sets quotas across all congressional districts in the state—a key and often overlooked step. She does not permit client time and budget pressures to influence her method. She is a rare pollster who uses the necessary time in the field for a poll to work.

Selzer refuses to believe in the "art" of polling. She does not view it as an art. Selzer has learned to ignore her intuition.

Her sampling frame is a list of registered voters. This list differs from a random digit dialing (RDD) approach many pollsters use. An RDD approach can capture those that have not registered yet and might vote. Unfortunately, RDD also captures people not registered and who will not vote.[89] Conversely, using a registered voter list can miss voters who may choose to register in the future, which is an issue in states with same-day voter registration like Iowa.

Selzer's secret weapon is how she predicts who will show up to vote. She does not have a traditional likely voter model. Most pollsters predict voter turnout by looking at prior elections

---

89   Surveying registered voters misses those that register late or on Election Day.

and assuming certain demographic groups, as well as liberals, independents, and conservatives will turn out as they have in the past. They model future turnout based on past information.

Modeling to the past works to the extent that the future looks like the past. But as Daniel Cassino wrote in the *Harvard Business Review* after the 2016 election, this approach does not work if voting trends change:

> It may be the case that standard sampling and weighting techniques are able to correct for sampling problems in a normal election—one in which voter turnout patterns remain predictable—but fail when the polls are missing portions of the electorate who are likely to turn out in one election but not in previous ones.[90]

Selzer does not weight to the past, as most pollsters do. She ignores historical voting trends when predicting who will turn out in the next election. She trusts Iowans to tell her if they will vote.

Her methods are forward looking. They swim against a tendency that marketers and pollsters have: to assume past data can predict the future. Douglas Rushkoff writes in his book *Present Shock*:

> No matter how invasive the technologies at their disposal, marketers and pollsters never come to terms with the living process through which people choose products or candidates; they are

---

90   Daniel Cassino, "Why Pollsters Were Completely and Utterly Wrong," *Harvard Business Review*, November 9, 2016, https://hbr.org/2016/11/why-pollsters-were-completely-and-utterly-wrong.

looking at what people just bought or thought, and making calculations based on that after-the-fact data.[91]

Selzer's critics try to paint Iowa as a specific environment. The
Iowa Poll has a trusted brand, so Iowans answer it faithfully. A
disproportionate amount of attention is paid to Iowa during
campaigns. Opinions are well formed. Iowans are different.
Midwestern people are more honest and cooperative than the
rest of the country.

The notion that Iowa is a unique environment does not hold
up when we examine what polling critics say happened in 2016.
One of the most common criticisms was that state-level polls in
the upper Midwest (Michigan, Wisconsin) were off. It is hard to
understand why the Iowa Poll nailed its prediction while polls
in Michigan and Wisconsin did not. These states have far more
similarities than differences.

If true, lessons lurk in these criticisms. Selzer's polls work
because she has established trust with people, and in turn, they
reply honestly and at higher rates. That is a situation more pollsters should seek to emulate rather than criticize.

I listened to a podcast where the director of a well-known college polling center began by boasting about his LVM. As a test,
he wanted to see if the Selzer approach would work with his
data. In four of five states he polled in, the Selzer approach
(trusting people to tell you if they will take the time to vote)
yielded the same estimate as his LVM approach (using dozens
of variables in an unexplainable logistic regression model). The

91   Douglas Rushkoff, *Present Shock: When Everything Happens Now* (London: Penguin, 2013).

one state that did not match came closer to the popular vote using the more straightforward Selzer approach.

Selzer's success—despite not focusing on past behavior to predict the future—underscores a fundamental problem in how pollsters reacted after 2016. The post-2016 polling confabs concluded that pollsters failed to take education level into sufficient account when predicting turnout. Pollsters adjusted their models to account for education. The result was voter turnout models for the 2020 election that likely would have done a great job in 2016 but failed in 2020.

Although all election years are unique, it does not take a genius to realize that 2020 was special because of the COVID-19 pandemic. Corporate research clients who had tracking studies going for years questioned the relevance of norms and benchmarks gathered before the spring of 2020 because the pandemic may have permanently changed consumer behavior.

Pollsters failed to see that the 2020 electorate was not the same as in 2016. Why? Having attended many post-2016 polling events and symposia, I can confirm that the people leading them were brilliant statisticians and methodologists. Methodologists are fascinating to talk to, and I have learned much from them over the years.

They are also "ivory tower" individuals not particularly attuned to the outside world. Seeing what is happening in the outside world makes the difference in a successful LVM.

Selzer has mastered this. Her "turnout model" is not backward looking. It focuses on asking the respondent if they will turn out. She presumes nothing.

In an interview about how her method differs from others, Selzer summarizes methodologists' tendencies to overcomplicate:

> My approach is probably the most simplistic of any of these polling firms. And so there's perhaps a commercial advantage to having a complicated scheme that makes people think it's all science-y and therefore it's better and it is secret and it's protected by patents and trademarks and all of that. Mine looks like a second grader dreamed it up, by comparison.[92]

I disagree with characterizing Selzer's approach as less "science-y" than others. Her approach has worked because it makes no assumptions. It takes the art out of polling.

The Selzer approach is the scientific one. I do not think a second grader could dream it up, but I believe a junior analyst at a market research firm could.

Selzer and her media partner (*The Des Moines Register*) are not shy about releasing a poll that does not conform to what other polls are saying. The final Iowa Poll in the 2020 race looked different than other polls in Iowa. Selzer has enough faith in her methods to release her polls when her results conflict with what other pollsters find. History has proved her right more than wrong.

Market researchers can learn from the Selzer approach to keep-

92 Mary Harris, "How the Polls Got the Election Wrong, according to One Pollster Who Got It Right," Slate, November 12, 2020, https://slate.com/news-and-politics/2020/11/iowa-election-polls-ann-selzer.html.

ing things simple. As a college professor once told me, "Smart people like to overcomplicate things."

Pre-election polls have drifted recently for many reasons, many of which are technical and complex. Complex issues do not necessarily need complex solutions. Usually, the simpler explanation is best.

CHAPTER 6

WHY POLLS GO BAD

EVERY SURVEY WEIGHTING ACTION
HAS AN OPPOSITE REACTION

Nonresearchers have a difficult time wrapping their heads around why data are weighted. Do you mean to tell me pollsters might count my response less than somebody else's? Yup. It happens all the time. Because we live in a world where probability sampling does not exist, we must weight data.

Weighting data is like playing with Silly Putty®. Remember Silly Putty? It was a popular toy that could do all sorts of things. It bounced. It could glue two objects together. Astronauts used it to secure tools while in space. If you left it alone on a warm day, it melted, and it was impossible to get out of your clothing and hair.

A remarkable property of Silly Putty was that if you flattened it and pressed it against a newspaper, it would transfer the image to the Silly Putty.

Imagine your survey data is a flattened handful of Silly Putty. Your task is to represent a one-panel comic from the newspaper with it. If your survey sample is plentiful and covers the image perfectly, this requires you to be careful as you press it against the comic.

Voilà, you have represented your universe! (Okay, it will be a mirror image, but ignore that!)

But this is not how Silly Putty or survey data work. What tended to happen was, there was not enough putty to flatten onto the newspaper, or it was not possible to cover the entire comic with it. You spread it out as best you could. After lifting the putty, you stretched it to make it look like the original or intentionally distort it.

When the putty was pressed in one direction, there tended to be a contraction in another. It was fun because you usually ended up with a funny image of your favorite comic character.

That is analogous to what researchers do to make a nonrandom sample match a universe. There may not be a big enough sample size (not enough putty), or some groups may be underrepresented (the putty cannot cover the comic perfectly). Through careful weighting (stretching the putty), we can get an imperfect but accurate enough representation of the universe (the comic). The universe (the comic) is distorted if we weight the data (stretch the putty). That is funny with Silly Putty but not so amusing with research data.

As "silly" as this sounds, it is a helpful analogy. Methodologists often weight data too much. Overweighting data is like stretching the Silly Putty until the comic becomes unrecognizable.

A researcher needs to know what the universe looks like, just as the Silly Putty user needs to know what the image they want to represent looks like—stretching it in the dark meets with poor results. And when one group is weighted (pull the putty in one direction), it has the effect of distorting another (push the putty in another direction).

Weighting is best used to make subtle adjustments to improve the picture. It is necessary because random samples do not exist. But it can be overdone.

Researchers have to be careful not to stretch the Silly Putty too far.

THERE ARE MANY ERRORS ON POLLS BEYOND THE ONES METHODOLOGISTS TRY TO FIX

This book began with a quotation from Humphrey Taylor that implied the potential for error on a poll is infinite. I am not sure I would go that far, but small mistakes make a difference when conducting a poll. These errors are inconsequential for many survey research projects. For pre-election polls, these errors may be the source of the few points they are off by.

Most analyses of polling mistakes concentrate on measurable statistical errors—issues such as sampling bias, weighting, and problematic likely voter models. The people who look into polling mistakes are statisticians, so they look to what they know. We will cover the statistical errors as well as practical issues that affect surveys and polls.

Dozens of people are involved in a polling project within a polling firm. Human errors happen along the way. Although good research firms have processes in place to guard against slipups, they do occur. Regularly.

HOW DOES A POLL REALLY GET DONE?

It is helpful to outline how a polling project gets done. Mistakes and errors happen at every point in this process.

THE SURVEY RESEARCH PROCESS

1. The client (the media, a campaign) contacts the research firm (pollster) and decides they want to do a study.
2. The pollster works with the clients to develop the study's objectives.
3. The pollster presents a proposal to the client, which outlines the project specifications, costs, and timing.
4. The researcher composes a questionnaire. This questionnaire is reviewed and redrafted until the client is happy with it.
5. This questionnaire is programmed for use on a survey system. This step involves coding, testing, running random data through the system to look for problems, and for online polls, reviewing the user experience on both mobile and desktop versions.
6. For an online poll, a sampling firm brings traffic to the questionnaire. Survey responders are obtained in various ways, the most common being an opt-in panel of potential respondents. For a telephone poll, a sampling firm provides a list of "seed" telephone numbers used to launch a random digit dialing process.
7. While the study is fielding, the sampling firm and the programmers watch progress toward the quotas the researcher established. They adjust traffic coming to the questionnaire. Poor-quality respondents are removed from the dataset at this stage, using both automated and subjective processes.
8. The programmer produces summary tables that show results question by question across demographic groupings.

9. The researcher takes this data and works with a methodologist to weight the data demographically and apply a likely voter model. This weights each person who responded to the survey by a prediction of their likelihood of voting.
10. The researcher composes a report for the client. The client publishes the poll, and the media uses it in its punditry.

Subjectivity is inherent at every stage of this process. Humans make decisions and mistakes at every step.

It is helpful to keep this process in mind as potential errors in surveys and polls are outlined. We have divided a discussion of these errors into five categories that we discuss in the next chapter:

1. Errors that take place at the design and specification stages
2. Errors specific to sampling/sample bias
3. Errors that take place while fielding studies
4. Errors that take place when analyzing data
5. Errors specific to the 2016 and 2020 polls

Before outlining specific issues that arise, it is essential to recognize an "uber" issue that pervades pre-election polling. Polling is a poor business proposition. As most polling organizations are for-profit firms, the resulting financial pressures cause many mistakes.

WHY IS POLLING SUCH LOUSY BUSINESS?

Pollsters have a hidden secret: polling is unprofitable, and financial pressures affect the quality of published polls.

A polling "insider" related the following troubling story to me.

After the 2004 election, he was called into a meeting with his CEO and CFO. They projected spreadsheets up on a screen that showed that his polling work failed to break even that year. They told him to return in a week with a plan for turning this business around.

He came back in a week and argued that opinion polling work should not be expected to turn a profit—that breaking even would be a good result. This opinion poll was well known, and he felt the focus should be on quality because his opinion polls built the firm's brand for its other business.

His CEO disagreed and decided, on the spot, to stop doing all opinion polling work and transfer some of his best people to other teams in the company. This firm was out of the opinion polling business for six months until a new CEO reversed this decision.

It takes a leader with vision to see that opinion polling is not such a great business but creates opportunities for the rest of the company. Financial pressures are paramount in most polling firms.

Polls done for political candidates are a losing business proposition. Campaigns are notorious for paying late. If you conduct a poll for a political candidate, there is perhaps a 50% chance of getting paid and maybe a 25% chance of being paid everything owed to you.

My company does not conduct polls for candidates because clients count on us to be neutral observers of the data we collect. It is not a good look to seem to favor one candidate or party over another.

Our clients are people with political views—if we pick a side, we will anger half of them. We would refuse to work for candidates even if this was not the case. Who wants to work for people who cannot be counted on to pay?

Reputable pollsters have the same view and will not work for candidates. Campaigns have a hard time getting good pollsters to work for them. The pollsters they do find are hyperpartisan. They are not impartial arbiters of the data they analyze. As a result, candidates can receive lousy advice from their internal polling.

Some of the best polls are conducted for the media and by college polling centers. Even partisan media, such as Fox News and MSNBC, have excellent polling divisions and partners. They have the proper incentive to get their polls right. Major media organizations have the resources to attract talent to their polling desks.

Having a media partnership is a big deal for pollsters. It builds their brands for their market research business. Although polling is rarely profitable, market research is.

Polling struggles to turn a profit because pollsters compete for these media partnerships. Many are willing to do polling projects below their cost. Polling is a marketing expense. Polls are a loss leader for most polling firms.

Some of the best research being done is by small, boutique firms like mine. But almost none of the polling work is being done by small firms. We do not have enough other work to offset the financial problems that polling work would cause.

The firm I first worked for[93] was *USA Today's* pollster. At that time, this newspaper was best known for being printed in color and being widely read by people traveling on business. In most hotels I stayed in, a copy of *USA Today* was slid under my door each morning.

USA Today was famous for its pie charts. On most days, a simple diagram was shown on a current topic of interest in the lower left-hand corner of the front page. The data for this graph were often provided by the polling company I worked for, whose name appeared underneath it.

We were a small company with a growing national reputation, but many clients had never heard of us. I attended numerous meetings with potential clients where I would show them the day's newspaper and point out our company's name on the front page.

This gave us instant credibility and positioned us to win many projects. Our *USA Today* partnership was a source of pride to our employees.

Pollsters understand the value of these media partnerships to their research business. This is why they bid against each other to get these media partnerships, and the result is the polling business runs on very thin margins.

Why is this a problem? Not having a proper budget in place creates difficulties for a research project. Research and polling companies are small. Most have a few dozen employees. The

---

93   The Gordon S. Black Corporation.

largest ones employ a few hundred. Only a handful have more than a thousand employees.

Folks at research and polling firms work hard. Research projects are deadline driven. With dozens of projects going on simultaneously, there are always a few approaching a deadline. It is a stressful job that involves many nights and weekends.

Internally, the attention projects receive follows the "invisible hand" of the budgets available for them. Most profit generated in research companies accrues from a handful of its best clients; 80% of their profit is likely being made from 20% of their clients. Those 20% are the clients and projects that attract the most resources and the most senior people. Polls rarely fall into this 20%.

Polling work is often up for debate at these firms. The accounting department wonders why the firm bothers with work that takes so much time and contributes so little to the bottom line. CEOs, especially if the company is publicly held, look at the short-term benefits of no longer doing polling work instead of the long-term benefits of building the firm's brand reputation.

The Gallup Organization, the organization that pioneered pre-election polling, no longer does them. Gallup chose to suspend its pre-election polls after 2012. The potential damage to their reputation from bad polls was not worth the money Gallup made (or did not make) on them.

In the polling world, this is as if McDonald's decided to stop selling hamburgers or Procter & Gamble stopped making Tide.

Budget pressures cause those working on the polls to react by doing what they can to make polls profitable. Staff spend less time on them, cut corners in the field, tack polling questions onto other studies, and try to deflect the attention of senior management away from the poll's finances.

Bad polls are not an inevitable result of financial pressures. But the internal incentives of a for-profit polling firm are misplaced when an underfunded project is conducted on too fast of a time frame. Nobody is promoted or given a raise for running an excellent pre-election poll.

Fortunately for the polls, most researchers are intrinsically motivated. What makes researchers unmanageable from a CEO's perspective is precisely what makes them good at their jobs. The brightest researchers I have known are involved in opinion polling. But they have to finagle themselves into working on these polls. Market forces push them to work on more profitable commercial research projects. Polling firms enjoy the attention the polls provide but dislike most other aspects.

CHAPTER 7

MISTAKES MADE EARLY IN THE PROCESS

IN MARKETING, GETTING IT DONE QUICKLY AND 90% RIGHT IS OFTEN GOOD ENOUGH

Specification errors have increased in research projects as time frames have compressed.

My firm has Silicon Valley clients with businesses moving and growing so fast that they are loose in defining their goals. These clients are often not entirely sure what they are trying to learn from a study or what they will do with the results, but they know they need customer input to make sound decisions and appease their investors.

This type of client demands speed over everything else. We have conducted projects that proceed through all 10 steps of the survey research process in about a week. Although researchers do their best to maintain quality, there are bound to be unseen errors in these projects.

I once had a client who was the CEO of a dot-com firm in Europe. He flew to

New York to meet with me, and we spent lunch together talking about the challenges his business faced launching in the United States. When we got back to our offices, he wrote me a check for $50,000 and told me he would be back in a month and wanted to see a market research report that addressed the issues we discussed at lunch.

I was nervous. He would not have any contact with me or have any input on the study. And I had forgotten to bring a pen and paper to our lunch meeting.[94]

For this type of client, there is something to be said for getting it 90% right and getting it done tomorrow. This approach works in these cases. These clients do not have the time to get it perfect. Getting their research done and gleaning fast insights is what they desire. Their data does not need to be precise.

This mentality is starting to permeate polling. Speed is becoming valued at the expense of quality. My firm is rewarded for getting things done quickly more than getting things done correctly.

This approach is not appropriate for polling. A slight miss can make or break a poll.

Errors that take place up front affect every survey, yet they are rarely discussed as potential reasons polls miss their election predictions. Let us dive into them.

PROBLEMS IN STUDY SPECIFICATION, TIMING, OR BUDGET

Errors early in any process magnify and create issues down the line. In survey research, it is common to discover that the

---

94   This client ended up happy with our work and launched in the United States later that year. His business was later acquired by Google.

underlying problems for a poor-quality study are that either (1) objectives were not well outlined, or (2) the study did not have a sufficient budget or time frame.

Specification errors are preventable and common. They affect every project because there is no such thing as an infinite budget and time frame.

There is an adage in project management that clients have three considerations on any project—the project can be fast, be good, or be cheap. The client can pick two of these. The project can be fast and good, but it will not be cheap. It can be fast and cheap, but it will not be good. Or it can be good and cheap, but then it will not be fast.

This concept is true of polls. Clients once demanded that their polls be good and cheap. As a consequence, projects would take a long time. Now speed is valued over most other considerations.

SPEED KILLS (A POLL)

With the rise of online data collection, clients prefer studies to be fast and cheap, and this has damaged quality. Polls have become much quicker and less expensive, but they have not become higher quality.

Every pre-election poll proceeds on a timeline that makes it impossible to prevent errors from occurring—every single one.

These rushed timelines are understandable. Real-world events move quickly. Clients want to know impacts on the likelihood of winning the election. The media will not wait weeks to report on the implications of nominating conventions, debates, or candidate gaffs; they move immediately. The media pressure pollsters to complete their work in a few days.

Pollsters cannot field a high-quality poll this quickly, especially one that must be as precise as a pre-election poll. It is not a matter of how hard the pollster works or how many people they put on the project. Unfixable errors occur by going too fast.

Say that you and I have both joined an online research database (panel) used for polling work. I am tethered to my online life and constantly on my computer and mobile phone for work and pleasure. You have a richer off-line life and hop online every couple of days. A poll conducted too quickly is more likely to interview people like me than people like you. I am online and waiting to be directed to an online survey while you are inaccessible until the next time you log on. That might be after the study has ended.

This matters. Online-centric people are more politically engaged, more educated, and more liberal in their thinking than those who are not.[95]

Although rushed polls can meet their demographic targets, they contain psychographic biases that are difficult to address. Good pollsters understand this. But even these pollsters create undiscovered biases that arise from fielding too fast. The core problem is not about weighting; it is about going too fast.

95   Shelley Boulianne, "Does Internet Use Affect Engagement? A Meta-analysis of Research," *Political Communication* 26, no. 2 (2009): 193–211, https://www.tandfonline.com/doi/pdf/10.1080/10584600902854363.

I suspect speed is at the heart of the 2020 polling miss. Polls were fielded too quickly to account for the Republican nonresponse bias.

UP TO HALF OF POLL RESPONDENTS ARE FAKING IT

Another issue that arises by going too fast is an increasing need to remove poor-quality respondents from the sample. It is harder to do this effectively when the study is fielded too quickly.

Just 10 years ago, researchers would need to remove 5%–10% of all interviews from online samples because of poor quality. That proportion is now in the 35%–50% range.

You read that correctly: up to half of all people who answer a poll have their answers removed from the dataset for quality issues. Later, this issue is outlined in more detail as it is a significant reason why the polls are not nailing their election predictions.

We counsel clients that studies should be in the field for *at least* 10 days, wrapping two weekends. Studies *should be* in the field for three weeks. That works well for the bulk of market research projects. It is an unworkable timeline for election and opinion polls.

Some pollsters field pre-election polls continuously to guard against these issues. A continuous survey interviews a small sample of people daily. It uses the daily data to create a weekly rolling average line. Ongoing data collection is an excellent way to conduct pre-election polls. It is not done much because it is costly, and the rolling nature of continuous data mutes the effect of specific events on the race.

BUDGET PRESSURES ARE EVERYWHERE IN POLLS

Another error is an insufficient budget or the pollster being under too much pressure to perform their work profitably. Researchers are under pressure to do good work and perform this work profitably. Polling is a *business* with all the accompanying pressures that come with that.

Polling pioneers, particularly Gallup, Roper, and Crossley, were disparaged by the academic community because they were private enterprises seeking to make a profit. In the minds of academics, pollsters could not fairly conduct their opinion polling work because of their business interests.

Budget pressures are particularly pronounced at larger research firms and publicly held firms. These firms have an incentive to take on every project that comes to them and finish them in the least amount of time using the most junior staff possible. It is like a law firm in that the client hires the partner, and the partner does all they can to delegate the work to the firm's junior staff.

When working in a major polling firm, I led a team that simultaneously worked on 20–50 projects at various stages. There were 15 teams like mine in the firm. Company-wide, there were likely about 500 concurrent projects. The projects receiving senior-level attention were the most profitable ones. They largely ignored the pre-election polls.

A project budget can be too big. I have had clients come to me with a project idea and tell me they have a budget that is double or triple what is needed for the study. Having an unlimited budget might sound like an ideal situation, but it is not. Having a budget is essential because constraints force decisions about priorities and objectives. A "blank check" causes the client to want to throw everything they can think of into the project. This situation occurs with market research studies, but I do not believe it ever has happened in polling work.

SMALL ERRORS MAKE A DIFFERENCE

Errors that come up at the project specification phase (defining objectives, setting the timeline, agreeing on a budget) are potentially big enough to explain all the pre-election polling misses. That sentence can be written about other errors as well.

Errors are not always in the same direction and can cancel each other out. Although Humphrey Taylor is correct in that the potential for errors may be infinite, many compensate for each other, so net errors are small.

This discussion of errors should not imply that survey researchers do not conduct high-quality studies. They do. Market research firms are efficient. I have worked with academic researchers who are in awe at how quickly we design, field, and analyze a study. This process takes market researchers weeks, where it takes academics years.

Good researchers realize the potential for errors. They bring other data sources into their analyses, look at prior research, and augment their studies with qualitative methods like focus groups and interviews. They will not base a meaningful conclusion on a single data point. Instead, they look for areas where data converge. They design projects to provide many data "angles" on important issues.

Election pollsters do not have this luxury. They are judged on a single data point: how close they came to predicting the victor. Pollsters rarely look at other data sources or other data points to triangulate their conclusions as market researchers do.

POOR QUESTIONNAIRE WORDING AND DESIGN IS HARD TO SPOT

I rarely know if I have written a poor question for an online survey. No interviewer is there to scold me. I do not hear a respondent's confusion.

I am lucky my telephone research experience has given me this perspective. Something has been lost in this for newer researchers who exclusively design online questionnaires. It is harder to empathize with someone when you do not hear their response.

An unmeasurable error source can ruin a study as much as improper weighting and sampling. When researchers ask a poorly designed question, they still receive an answer. A piece of data ambles into the database. Although good analysts may sometimes notice the problem, no statistical test can indicate if the information is accurate.

The move to online research and the increase in project speed have magnified this source of error. Sometimes clients are attuned to their internal business needs but do not know their customer base all that well. They pressure research agencies to ask unanswerable questions.

Many survey questions are poorly worded, and the analyst does not realize people are answering what they (respondents) interpret as the question. The analyst assumes respondents are answering what they (the analyst) meant for the question to ask. Sometimes these are not the same, and the analysis may be wrong.

I will provide an example. About five years ago, I worked on a project for a consumer-packaged goods client in a low-involvement category. The product was inexpensive (it sold for less than $3) and ubiquitous—more than 90% of Americans owned it.

It was not very interesting and was bought on a price basis. More than two-thirds of the category volume was private label. For all intents, the category was a commodity purchased on a price basis.

Our client wanted to delve into the consumer's mindset when buying and using the product. They devised a list of 36 product characteristics. Our task was to discover which characteristics differentiated their product from the competition and drove sales.

This is a common project objective, but it was unworkable for this particular product.

The reason? The product was inexpensive, and customers rarely thought about it, let alone its performance on 36 nuanced characteristics. I had never heard of at least half of the attributes despite using the product my entire life. We were asking customers to differentiate traits they had not considered in advance.

We built a questionnaire and conducted a study. We found the

36 items were highly correlated with each other. We applied a statistical test[96] that showed that consumer opinion came down to recognizing the brand, how sweet it tasted, and how much it cost.

There were only three questions to ask, yet we had posed 36. The disappointed client did not hire us again.

It took me months to understand why this study failed. I finally understood that writing a good question is like brain surgery without the mess. One way to view the questionnaire writing task is to recognize we are trying to get inside a person's brain and retrieve an opinion. Retrieving an established view works well for high-involvement decisions and issues where a person has thought about the topic in advance.

Suppose we want to find out how much someone likes their job, how they view their local school district, or what color they feel the sky is. We are conducting simple brain surgery—going inside their brains and plucking out an established opinion via a carefully worded question. It works well.

If we ask questions on topics that people have never considered before, there is nothing in the brain to retrieve. We create an observer effect. People have not considered 36 different characteristics for inexpensive products.

Our study asked them to discover an obscure attribute, develop an opinion, and express it in about 10 seconds. We did this 36 times!

---

96   Factor analysis.

People provide an answer, but an enormous amount of error is involved. Our measures are not reliable.

In short, when you ask a question, you get an answer. That does not mean the answer is meaningful or accurate. Low-involvement products are low risk. They involve little consequence of making a "wrong" decision.

Consumers apply more heuristic approaches in these situations. As pollsters, we are placing people in a position where they must think fast when we should measure how they think slowly.[97]

The more we try to retrieve already-established thoughts on surveys, the more accurate and valuable the data are. We can still research low-involvement products, but we must pose questions a person can answer meaningfully.

Researchers should appreciate that consumers' lives are hectic. Settling on a limited number of easily understandable decision criteria for low-involvement items is how the consumer world works.

In the end, if consumers contemplated 36 attributes in the real world, the product would have sold for a much higher price. It was not worth their time to consider a $3 purchase in this much detail. There is no risk in getting the decision wrong.

Plenty of textbooks[98] cover common problems in question

---

97   This is an important concept for pollsters. I would recommend Daniel Kahneman's *Thinking, Fast and Slow* (New York: Farrar, Straus and Giroux, 2011).

98   Gilbert A. Churchill and Dawn Iacobucci, *Marketing Research: Methodological Foundations* (Nashville: South Western Educational Publishing, 2006).

design, such as double-barreled questions, leading questions, question order affecting results, and so forth. These problems do occur, but most researchers know about them and work hard to prevent them. The talent in questionnaire design is more about translating a client's objectives into a line of questioning that works for the people we survey.

Although questionnaire design issues are problematic in market research studies, they are not significant sources of errors in pre-election polls. Questions posed in pre-election polls are well established. Most pollsters use the same wording for key questions. The "horse race" question is placed early in the questionnaire, so there is little chance of order and fatigue biases. Because question wording for pre-election polls is similar across pollsters, it is unlikely to be a cause of why different polls can get different results.

POLLSTERS ARE HUMAN AND MAKE MISTAKES

Humans make decisions and mistakes at every step in research. Years ago, I asked my largest client why she kept commissioning so many studies with us. She replied, "Most firms I contract with screw up about one in every three projects I give to them. You seem to screw up one in 20 of them."

Although that sounds flippant, there is truth to her comment. Market research projects go awry more often than any of us would like to admit.

I was often reactive when I led a team of researchers at a major polling firm. This team fielded hundreds of projects each year. There were typically a few with serious problems I had to address. We had talented people on our team and in our company. We had processes to prevent errors, yet human errors happened, as they do in any business.

A small, human mistake can affect the data. These mistakes are hard to spot. In a single missed keystroke, a programmer can improperly weight a dataset. Honest programming mistakes have caused people to skip entire lines of questioning. I have received datasets where the men were coded as women and vice versa, resulting from a programmer mistyping one number in a line of code.

Errors that cause these types of mistakes are tiny. Many go unnoticed. I know researchers who hate tracking polls because they uncover minor errors that we fail to notice with one-time projects.

Between 15 and 50 people have a role in conducting a typical poll. This includes the client, a few people on the pollster's project staff, people at the sampling firm, programmers, data processors, coders, methodologists, and quality control personnel. Add in another 10–20 interviewers if it is a telephone poll.

That makes for considerable potential for human error along the way. Despite the scientific aura surrounding research, it suffers from human mistakes that affect any business. Pollsters have processes to prevent and catch human errors, but these mistakes can still occur.

These "human" mistakes go unrecognized as a potential source of errors on polls. Instead, those assessing the polls hone in on one particular error: sampling error. Sampling error is measurable and fixable, when discovered. But it is hardly the sole explanation for why polls can miss their marks.

CHAPTER 8

SAMPLING AND SAMPLE BIASES

A TINY MISTAKE CAN RUIN AN ENTIRE POLL

In 1993, the firm I worked for conducted a poll for a suburban village government. This village was considering establishing a police department. The possible creation of a police department was contentious within the village. Officials were concerned that they only heard from the loudest voices during town hall meetings.

They called us in to conduct an opinion poll. Should the village create a police department or continue using (and paying for) the county sheriff's department?

This village was unique in that it was geographically split in half by the Erie Canal. It was initially settled on the north side of the canal. The housing stock on that side was historical, the neighborhoods were mature and quiet, and residents were conservative in their outlook.

Neighborhoods were newer on the canal's south side. The bulk of that area had been developed in the past two decades. Its residents were younger, more likely to have children, and more liberal than the "northsiders."

We bought a random digit dial (RDD) "seed" sample for our telephone survey. This village had four local telephone exchanges, and this allowed us to use a list that randomized the telephone number's last four digits—a standard procedure in polling.

We completed the study smoothly. Our CEO presented the results to the village board. It showed overwhelming support for the creation of a new police department.

During the question-and-answer session, a dozen people came forth to say they did not believe the poll results because neither they nor their neighbors had been called.

Our CEO came back from the meeting and asked us to look closer at the sampling.

It turns out our programmer had made a tiny but consequential mistake. Instead of using the command for "randomize," she had inserted a command for "numerical order" into the program.

Instead of dialing telephone numbers randomly, this caused the survey system to call telephone numbers in sequential order. The two phone exchanges covering the north side of the village started with "2," while the exchanges covering the south side of the village began with "3" and "4."

The result is we called half the area and had ignored the other half. The half of the village we called just happened to be the half that most supported the creation of a police department. We had to redo the poll from scratch.

One honest mistake in a line of code created a gigantic mess.

Sampling is central to polling. A pollster can get projectible data within a known error rate by carefully selecting who is invited to a poll. Unfortunately, sampling errors are frequent and have become more prevalent.

POTENTIAL SAMPLING ERRORS

Sampling errors on pre-election polls are well studied. Most postmortem seminars I attended after the 2016 and 2020 elections focused on sampling problems. Methodologists, the media, and other observers concentrate on sampling errors to the exclusion of other errors. For example, AAPOR's 2016 postmortem implied that improper sampling caused problems with the 2016 polls.

Pollsters are myopic about potential sampling errors. It is what they focus on because sampling errors are measurable, and it is "what they know." A polling firm sounds intelligent when they trot out their methodologists to outline complicated sampling methods and statistics.

Sampling errors are not all that large in presidential pre-election polls, but tiny errors matter in close elections decided by a few percentage points. They are not to be ignored. I tell our clients that we can usually recover if we fail to ask a question or pose a poorly worded question on a study, but if we ask questions of the wrong people, we are in trouble.

Pollsters think that because polls are off by a little, tweaking the sampling a little will fix the problem. I am more of the view that there are many potential sources of error, these errors constantly change, and they can cancel each other out. Focusing on a single mistake is not going to cure the polls.

The problems that come with focusing solely on sampling issues are proven in the real world. Sampling errors of 2016 were addressed by the 2020 polls, which performed worse than the 2016 polls.

One type of sampling error relates to differential responses based on political party affiliation. In the late 1980s, most polls were conducted by telephone with live interviewers. Good researchers were mindful of not going too quickly in polls—to process "callbacks," which are calls made to recontact people who were not available.

The reason? Telephone interviews overrepresented Republicans, who were seen as more likely to be at home, and underrepresented Democrats, who were more likely to be out of their homes on the nights and weekends when pollsters conducted telephone polls.

Remember, this was in the days of landline phones. If you were outside your home, you were unreachable to a pollster. A researcher's way to reach you was tethered to your home.

That thinking has changed as online polls have arisen and more people have chosen to answer polls on their mobile phones. Today's prevailing wisdom is that without correction, both online and telephone polls underrepresent Republicans, who are less technologically centered, and overrepresent Democrats, who have technology more at the center of their lives. Going too fast with a poll exacerbates this problem.

The differential partisan nonresponse bias is well known. Most pollsters take this into account. Pollsters balance data to have the right blend of Democrats, Republicans, and Independents in their final sample. That in itself is problematic, as it is akin to weighting on the variable you are trying to predict in a survey.

The current partisan nonresponse bias problem centers on the *type* of Democrat or Republican that answers polls. Early indications from polling experts are that most polls got the proportion of Republicans correct in 2020. What they did not consider is that not all Republicans are alike. Pollsters undersampled Republicans with strongly conservative views and those who live in rural areas.

This underrepresentation is at least a partial explanation for what went amiss with the 2020 polls—as polls underrepresented the most fervent Trump supporters, who may live in hard-to-reach areas and may not live a technologically centered life. Because of this, they overestimated Biden's support.

The Crux Poll showed that urbanicity (whether someone lives in a city, suburb, or rural area) strongly predicts trust in pollsters. Researchers are not addressing their tendency to ignore rural people.

Not all sampling biases are consequential. It is only the biases that correlate with voting behavior that influence making a good prediction. Correcting for other sampling biases creates more problems than it solves.

BIAS IS A MISUNDERSTOOD TERM

The polling community can claim the 2016 and 2020 polls were accurate because they picked the correct popular vote winner, and these pre-election polls were about as good or bad as polls have been historically.

This is true but ignores an essential issue regarding bias. I have paid close attention to conversations that discuss 2016 and 2020 polling performance. I have not heard even one expert discuss this particular issue.

Bias is a loaded word, and what it means in statistics is not what it means in real life.[99] In statistics, a biased estimate is systematically off. A classic example, which you see in textbooks, imagines a shooting range and a series of bull's-eye targets. Each target has 10 holes in it.

- The "reliability" measure is how close the 10 holes are to each other. A wide spread means the shooter is unreliable. If the holes are all tight together, the shooter is reliable.
- "Bias" refers to how far from the target's center the central point of the 10 shots is. Say the 10 shots clump together. If that clump is close to the bull's-eye, the shooter is unbiased. If this clump is far to one side, the shooter is biased, although they may be reliable.

The goal is to have both a reliable (all shots in the same place) and unbiased (the center of all shots is at the bull's-eye) shooter.

The 2016 and 2020 polls were reliable. All essentially predicted

---

99 Statisticians have done the world a disservice by using terms like "bias," "validity," "reliability," and "significance," which have different meanings in statistics than they do in the broader world.

the same thing. Also, they were accurate in the sense that the clump of shots was not far off the bull's-eye.

But the polls were biased (again, in the statistical sense). Nearly all were off in the same direction from the bull's-eye—in the Democratic candidate's favor.

If I were teaching a survey research course, I would use this bull's-eye example and follow it up with the performance of the US pre-election polls of 2016 and 2020. The performance of these polls matches a textbook definition of statistical bias.

Something is systematically off with US pre-election polling. Pollsters and trade groups have not discussed or addressed this. The public knows it for sure.

LIKE IN OTHER AREAS, THERE ARE SYSTEMIC BIASES IN SURVEY RESEARCH

There has been increasing attention on systemic biases in society's institutions. Typically, these biases work against people of color. Systemic bias refers to structures that either overtly or unknowingly create and perpetuate biases.

Survey research is no different in that systemic biases exist, but the field is unique in that researchers have long studied and tried to correct these issues.

In the absence of countermeasures, minority groups, particularly Black and African Americans, are underrepresented in surveys and opinion polls. Thus, minority opinions are often not adequately captured. A lack of minority representation in the polls feeds into a cycle of politicians not taking minority opinions into account when crafting policy. It also leads to poor election predictions.

Minorities are underrepresented in sampling frames, particularly in online surveys. Opinion polls rely on technology (telephones, smartphones, internet connection) to reach people. When a group has less of these technologies, the group will be underrepresented in polls. Compounding this is that most minority groups respond at lower rates as well.

Researchers have long realized this. It is typical to get about half as many Black people as their population distribution would suggest in an RDD telephone sample. So what researchers do is "over-quota" these groups. Rather than trusting the random sample to provide the correct balance of racial and ethnic minorities, quotas are set to ensure that the correct number are interviewed.

Setting racial and ethnic quotas is commendable, and pollsters have done this for decades. Even the poorest-performing pollsters take the time to develop proper quotas for racial and ethnic minorities.

The issue is not merely about getting minorities to answer polls. The minorities who choose to respond to a survey must represent those who do not respond. It is not necessarily the case that a person of color who decides to become part of an online panel and chooses to answer a poll has the same opinions as a person of color who chooses not to be part of this process. This nonresponse bias is true of all groups but is particularly problematic with minorities.

There is also an issue that most opinion polling firms do not have many people of color working for them. This lack of staff diversity is a problem worth resolving for a crucial reason: market researchers and pollsters are the folks providing the information to the rest of the world on diversity issues. Our field cannot possibly give decision makers a proper perspective if we are not more diverse ourselves. We are the ones who inform everyone else about public opinion on these issues.

Survey researchers must get this right. Policymakers and corporate leaders lean on survey research data to understand systemic biases. If there is a bias in the way researchers obtain the opinions of disaffected groups, it perpetuates these biases in society. As pollsters, we collect the data that decision makers use to address these biases. We need to be vigilant that we do not inadvertently inject our biases into these data.

To the pollsters' credit, this issue is well studied. Polling firms spend energy trying to address this problem, which is more than can be said for many institutions. Yet, the problem of systemic bias remains and needs recognition.

A BIAS IS NOT ALWAYS CONSEQUENTIAL IN SURVEY RESEARCH

All bias is terrible, right? Well, "bias" in the real-world sense has a negative connotation. But in statistics, not all biases are created equal. Some do not matter. There are no desirable statistical biases, but there are *inconsequential* biases.

All good researchers seek to minimize sampling bias in their studies. Few realize sampling biases may not matter. "Sampling bias" means that samples might fail to cover some groups or fail to cover them in their proper proportion.

For example, without setting quotas, most consumer studies conducted in the United States would end up with about two-thirds of survey responders who identify as women and one-third who identify as men. Women respond to survey invitations at nearly double the rate as men do. Without correction, this would skew results.

Known sampling biases are addressed by setting quotas, by weighting data on the back end, or with a combination of the two. I can assure you pollsters are doing this for the obvious groups—age groups, race/ethnicity, sex/gender, and so forth.

Many researchers (including experienced ones) fail to recognize these biases may or may not be relevant. A sampling bias will only change the findings if the groups respond differently to the questions.

Suppose, for example, that Biden's support among women and men was identical. In this case, the same prediction for his support level would be calculated whether 100% women, 100% men, or any combination between were interviewed. If a study inadequately samples one sex/gender, it will not matter to the prediction of who will win the election (in this example).

I tell clients that "if you are asking 'What color is the sky?' the bias in your sample will not matter much." When everyone answers the same way (blue), it does not matter who you interview. When there is a large expected variability between segments (such as when we are doing a pre-election poll), it does matter.

Methodologists fail to see this. They overweight data, which carries a statistical cost. There is no reason to weight on a criterion if the data do not vary on it. This weighting will not change the data. It will introduce yet another error.

My previous firm had outstanding methodologists. We were required to send our datasets off to the methodological team for weighting when data collection was completed. This process delayed projects. It could take up to a week to get the weighted data back since the methodological team was doing this for the entire company. Our project team would compose our report from the unweighted data and update it when the weighted data came back so we could deliver reports on time.

Over dozens of studies across many years, I cannot recall changing conclusions when reports were updated to incorporate the methodologists' work. Percentages tended to tweak by a point here or there. We were left wondering why we bothered to give them our data.

However, I remember when the complex weighting schemes the methodologists favored would throw off obvious parameters, like age and sex/gender. They would stretch the Silly Putty too far.

When you see differences between weighted and unweighted datasets, this is likely indicative of a problem lurking in the sampling for the project. This should set off further investigation.

I anecdotally noticed this, but it became more recognized later. In 2018, Pew released a report[100] that concluded, "Choosing the right variables for weighting is more important than choosing the right statistical method" and "the most basic weighting method… performs nearly as well as more elaborate techniques."[101]

In short, methodologists have overdone their weighting. They wield large statistical hammers and wander around organizations looking for nails. Methodologists hold considerable sway within research firms. They spend their days trying to kill all the snakes they see and often try to kill some snakes that are not even there. They do not realize the snake they need to slay is the one that will bite.

THE MYTH OF THE RANDOM SAMPLE

Sampling is at the essence of market research and polling. A few people are asked questions, and researchers assume everyone who was not surveyed would have answered the same way. Most pre-election polls ask about 1,000 people to state their voting intentions. Pollsters then project this result to the entire voting population (150 million people in 2020).

Sampling works in many contexts. Your doctor does not need to test all your blood to determine your cholesterol level—an ounce or two ounces will do, thankfully. Chefs taste a spoonful of their creations. They assume the rest of the pot tastes the same.

---

100 Andrew Mercer, Arnold Lau, and Courtney Kennedy, "For Weighting Online Opt-In Samples, What Matters Most?" Pew Research Center, January 26, 2018, https://www.pewresearch.org/methods/2018/01/26/for-weighting-online-opt-in-samples-what-matters-most/.

101 The benefit in using more complex weighting techniques is that they help identify what are the right variables to use in the first place. But the more complex techniques tend to get the same result as simple techniques if the same weighting variables are used.

Pollsters can predict an election by interviewing a small number of people using the same concept.

Mathematical procedures that enable researchers to project to a broader population assume a random sample. Or as I tell research analysts, everything they taught you in statistics assumes a random sample. *T*-tests, hypotheses tests, regressions, and so forth all assume you have a random sample.

Here is the problem: polls do not have random samples. I suppose it is possible to do, but over 30 years and 3,500 projects, I have not seen a single project that can honestly claim a random sample.

A random sample remains the Holy Grail for survey researchers.

A random sample is possible among a captive audience. A researcher can randomly sample the passengers on a flight or a few students in a classroom or prisoners in a detention facility. The math behind random sampling applies as long as you are not trying to project beyond that flight or classroom or jail.

Here is the more significant problem: Most pollsters do not recognize this, disclose this, or think through how to deal with it. Worse, many purport their samples are indeed random when they are not.

The telephone random digit dial (RDD) sample was once the standard approach. Telephone researchers could randomly dial landline numbers. Random calls provided excellent data when landline telephone penetration and response rates were high.

RDD methods were still not providing a genuinely random or

probability sample. Some households had more than one phone line (and few researchers corrected for this). Many people lived in group situations (colleges, medical facilities) where they could not be reached for surveys. Some households did not have a landline, and even at its peak, telephone response rates were only about 70%.

Not bad. But also not random.

Researchers were presented with new opportunities and challenges as the internet came of age. Telephone response rates plummeted (to 5%–10%),[102] making telephone research prohibitively expensive and of poor quality. Online, no national directory of email addresses or cell phone numbers[103] existed. There were legal prohibitions against spamming, so researchers had to find new ways to contact people for surveys.

Initially, and this is still the dominant method today, research firms created opt-in panels of potential respondents. Potential research participants joined a panel, filled out an extensive demographic survey, and were offered small incentives to participate in projects.

These panels suffer from three self-selection bias issues:

1. Not everyone is online or online with the same enthusiasm or frequency.

---

102 Courtney Kennedy and Hannah Hartig, "Response Rates in Telephone Surveys Have Resumed Their Decline," Pew Research Center, February 27, 2019, https://www.pewresearch.org/fact-tank/2019/02/27/response-rates-in-telephone-surveys-have-resumed-their-decline/.

103 Also, in the early days of cell phones, call recipients paid for the call as well as the caller. This affected compliance with surveys and polls.

2. Not everyone online wants to be in a survey research panel.

3. Not everyone in the panel will take part in a particular survey.

The result is a convenience sample. Researchers figured out sophisticated ways to handle the sampling challenges that result from panel-based samples.[104] These convenience samples can work well. But in no way are they a random sample.

River sampling is a term used to describe people "intercepted" on the internet and asked to fill out a survey. Potential poll takers are invited via online ads and offers placed on various websites. If interested, they are prescreened and sent along to the online questionnaire.

River samples should be used as a last resort. They are disruptive. They intercept people doing other things online, which affects their mindsets when answering surveys. River samples can target obscure research audiences because they use the same technologies that allow advertisers to target you online. The more active you are online, the greater contrails you leave that will enable researchers to target you. By definition, river samples skew toward highly active internet users.

Sampling firms have excellent science behind river sampling because so much is known about what people are doing online these days. It can work, but response rates are low, and the online world is changing fast, so it is hard to get a consistent

104 George Terhanian, John Bremer, Jonathan Olmsted, and Jiqiang Gu, "A Process for Developing an Optimal Model for Reducing Bias in Nonprobability Samples: The Quest for Accuracy Continues in Online Survey Research," *Journal of Advertising Research* 56, no. 1 (2016): 14–24, https://psycnet.apa.org/record/2016-15759-005.

river sample over time. An honest researcher would never use "random sampling" to describe river samples.

Panel-based and river samples represent how the lion's share of survey research is conducted today: fast and inexpensive. When used intelligently, these methods can approximate the findings of a random sample. Panel and river samples come "close enough" to a random selection for most market research studies. But not for pre-election polls.

These samples are far from perfect, but the companies providing them do not promote them as random samples. They involve biases. Researchers deal with these biases as best they can methodologically.

Too often, researchers forget that their data violate requirements for statistical tests: that the sample is random. Researchers fail to state that the statistical tests they use were not designed for the data they gather.

This brings us to a newer idea in the research sampling world: address-based samples (ABS). ABS are purer from a methodological standpoint. Although ABS have been around for some time, they are just now being used extensively in survey research.

ABS are based on United States Postal Service (USPS) lists. Because USPS has a list of all US households, this is an excellent sampling frame. (The Census Bureau and the IRS also have great lists, but they are not available for researchers to use.) The USPS list is the starting point for ABS.

Research firms will use the USPS list to enlist participants in a panel or entice people to participate in an individual study. This recruitment can be by mail, phone, or online. Publicly known information is often appended onto the list.

As you might expect, an ABS approach suffers from similar issues as other approaches. Cooperation rates are low, and payments to entice response (sometimes significant) are necessary. These payments can create biases.

Most ABS surveys are conducted online. Yet, not everyone on the USPS list is online or has the same level of online access. Some groups (undocumented immigrants, homeless people) may not be on the USPS list. Some (full-time RVers, college students, frequent travelers) are hard to reach.

ABS approaches do not cover rural areas as well as urban areas. Some households use post office boxes and not residential addresses for their mail. Others use more than one address. Although ABS lists cover about 97% of US households, the 3% they do not cover are not randomly distributed.

The good news is, if done correctly, biases that result from an ABS are more correctable than those from other samples because they are measurable. A recent Pew study shows that survey bias and the number of bogus[105] respondents is slightly smaller for ABS than opt-in panel samples.[106]

---

105 A "bogus" respondent refers to a fake respondent, usually one created by a bot or a scripted program. Bogus respondents have become a serious problem for market researchers and pollsters.

106 Courtney Kennedy, Nick Hatley, Arnold Lau, Andrew Mercer, Scott Keeter, Joshua Ferno, and Dorene Asare-Marfo, "Assessing the Risks to Online Polls from Bogus Respondents," Pew Research Center, February 18, 2020, https://www.pewresearch.org/methods/2020/02/18/assessing-the-risks-to-online-polls-from-bogus-respondents/.

ABS are not random samples either. It would be surprising if, among all those approached to participate in a study using an ABS, more than 10% end up in the panel. Just because the invitation to join was random does not mean the resulting sample is random.

The problem is not with ABS, as most researchers would concur ABS is the best current option and comes the closest to a random sample. Many firms providing ABS are selling them as "random samples." That is disingenuous. Just because the sampling frame used to recruit a survey panel can claim to be "random" does not mean the people who end up in a research database constitute a random sample.

Does this matter? In many ways, it likely does not. Biases and errors exist in all surveys. These biases and errors vary by how the study is sampled. They also vary by the topic of the questions, the survey's tone, survey length, and so forth. Many times, survey errors are not the same throughout an individual survey. Biases in surveys are "known unknowns"—we know they are there but are unsure what they are.

The improvement in bias achieved by an ABS over a panel-based sample is tiny. It is likely inconsequential when considered next to the other sources of error that can creep into a research project.

Because of this, and since ABS sampling is costly, we only recommend ABS panels in two cases: (1) if the study may result in academic publication, as academics are more accepting of data that comes from an ABS approach, and (2) if we are working in a small geography, where panel-based samples are not feasible.

ABS are likely the best available at this moment. But some firms inappropriately portray them as yielding random samples. The minor improvements in bias they provide are not worth the higher budget and expanded study time frame for most projects. ABS are currently used in a tiny proportion of research studies. ABS is "state of the art," with an emphasis on "art," as sampling is less of a science than people think.

Few pre-election polls use ABS. Why? Mainly because ABS take time to develop and are expensive. ABS cost 10 times more and take 10 times as long as online samples. It would be hard to find a polling client willing to pay for an ABS or take the time to develop one.

But some are moving in that direction. In 2021, CNN decided to change its polling methods to use ABS for its opinion polling. Several times a year, they plan to invest the time to develop an ABS and develop measures that are used as benchmarks for their pre-election and opinion polling. This is a step in the right direction.

POLLS OVERLOOK RURAL AMERICA

I have attended hundreds of focus groups. These are small group discussions led by a moderator among four to 12 participants. Sessions occur in a conference room decked with recording equipment and a one-way mirror. Increasingly, these sessions take place remotely using video conferencing tools.

During traditional focus groups, researchers and clients sit behind a one-way mirror in a relaxing, multitiered lounge. The lounge has comfortable chairs, a refrigerator with beer and wine, exercise equipment, and an insane number of M&Ms. Experienced researchers have learned to sit as far away from the M&Ms as possible.

Focus groups serve many purposes. Clients use them to test new product ideas or refine advertising messages. We recommend them to clients if their objectives are not ready for survey research. We sometimes like to do focus groups after a survey research project is complete, to put personality on the data and to have an opportunity to pursue unanswered questions.

There is a problem with focus groups that receives little attention. I would estimate that at least half of all focus groups are held in three cities: New York, Chicago, and Los Angeles. Most of the other half are held in other major cities or travel destinations like Las Vegas or Orlando.

These city choices can have little to do with the project objectives. Focus groups often occur near the client's offices or in easy-to-get-to cities. Clients sometimes choose locations because they want to go there.

The result is that early-stage product and advertising ideas are evaluated among urban or suburban participants who live in or near a large city. Smaller cities, small towns, and rural consumers are not afterthoughts in focus group research; they are rarely thought about *at all*.

Even when marketers attempt to hold focus groups among rural people, they are limited to those who live within an hour or so of a city because that is where the facilities are. Rural consumers who live farther from an urban area are omitted because it would take them too long to drive to the facility.

I have been conscious of this because I am from a rural village and have never lived in a major metropolitan area. The people I grew up with and knew best were not being asked to provide their opinions in focus groups. This issue happens with surveys and polls as well. Rural and small-town America are underrepresented.

Many years ago, I began adding items into questionnaires that would permit me to look at the differences between urban, suburban, and rural people. I would find differences, but pointing them out met with little excitement from clients who were uninterested in targeting their products or marketing to a small-town audience.

Underrepresenting rural America was less of an issue for quantitative market research and polling during the telephone research era, as RDD telephone samples could include rural residents.

Today's online samples do not include rural people as effectively as RDD telephone samples. Rural respondents in online sampling databases are not representative of all rural people, many of whom have relatively low levels of online activity. Weighting them upward does not make them representative.

Clients have never asked me to correct a sample to represent rural America. The result is products and services designed for suburbia. Marketers do not consider the specific needs of small-town folks.

The analog in polling is that the suburban voice is amplified while the rural voice is dampened.

Biases only matter if they affect what is being measured. If rural and suburban respondents feel the same way about something, this issue does not matter.

Yet, it *often does* matter. It can matter for product research. It matters to the educational research my firm conducts. It is likely a vital cause of the problems with pre-election polling.

The failure to adequately capture rural respondents creates a bias that can make or break a pre-election poll. As Fareed Zakaria wrote in 2020:

> The urban-rural divide, which is growing every year, might be the most significant fault line in America electorally speaking—more so than race or gender.[107]

Currently, it is rare for a pollster to balance their samples on urbanicity. There are statewide polls that do an excellent job of sampling across all election districts in the state, but even those do not pay attention to getting the proportion of rural respondents correct within those election districts.

Most pollsters are making this mistake. In 2016, the polls failed to sample voters in the lower education categories. In 2020, the polls failed to reach the most fervent Trump supporters. Figuring out how to get rural America to respond to polls is essential to getting predictions right.

---

107 Fareed Zakaria, *Ten Lessons for a Post-pandemic World* (London: Penguin, 2020).

HOW PEOPLE WHO RESPOND TO POLLS ARE FOUND: ONLINE PANELS AND SAMPLE MARKETPLACES

With online polls, a critical source of error creeps into projects right at the beginning. This error relates to how researchers source respondents.

All research studies and polls seek to understand something about a wider population. In a pre-election poll's case, this population is "adults who will vote in the election." The key to successful polling is to set a study up so that the list used (the sampling frame) matches the population as closely as possible.

Sampling frames never perfectly match the population of interest, but they can come close. RDD telephone samples used to come close to representing the entire US population. They would still miss those without phones or those living in group settings (such as college students reliant on one phone per residence hall). In the case of online research, there is potential for a greater mismatch of the sampling frames to the population.

Earlier, we discussed that online samples for polls are sourced from panels, via intercepts (also known as river sampling), and sometimes by ABS. These sources are too expensive to develop and maintain for all but a handful of large polling organizations. As a result, large companies that recruit and manage panels and river samples have arisen. Most polling is conducted by contracting with these companies to provide respondents.

Pollsters are all using the same sources to get people to take their surveys. If something is systematically wrong with the polls, we need to investigate these companies further.

Few researchers comprehend how sampling companies get panelists or river-based respondents. These companies are often a result of mergers and acquisitions of smaller companies, all of which have their own methods.

The resulting databases are unexplainable. I have had panelist company methodologists explain how they source their panelists. Their workflow diagrams looked like something from a Rube Goldberg cartoon. I am not sure the panel companies even know how their panelists are obtained.

Online research panels are crafted from an assortment of recruiting methods. People may have been obtained from a customer database. Others may have been intercepted online and invited to take part. Some may have joined a smaller panel and become part of a larger panel when a smaller company was acquired.

The result is a convenience sample. A convenience sample is not a random sample—it is a kind term that means researchers are dipping into a pool of conveniently available survey takers. Today, the lion's share of polling is conducted using convenience samples.

Convenience samples are not necessarily a bad thing. What matters is constructing a sample that is projectible to a larger population. The beauty of a random sample is its simplicity. When a sample is random, all the work is done for the researcher. With convenience samples, much more work is involved in making them representative of a wider population. Humans must intervene. And humans make mistakes.

Despite using convenience samples, panel companies do not supply poll takers willy-nilly. They have methodologists who study their samples' deficiencies and biases. They reach out to new sources of panelists to compensate for their deficiencies.

Convenience samples do not have to be low quality or unrepresentative. Convenience samples can be as accurate as random samples. But it is challenging to construct a workable convenience sample when the panel itself is sourced in such a complicated fashion.

Adding to this complexity is a recent development in research and polling called the sampling marketplace. A sampling marketplace pools the panels of many panel companies. A typical marketplace has a front-end interface for the researcher, who specifies the population they seek to research. A reverse-auction ensues, where various panel companies bid against each other to supply the panelists with the low bid winning. This process happens automatically through programs that allow different panel companies' computers to quickly assess their sample inventory. The result is the researcher can get survey respondents at a low price.

Sample marketplaces have solved the problem of getting fast and cheap samples, but they have sacrificed quality in the process.

One person I interviewed for this book told me that "sample marketplaces are all about speed, but it is like they think that if you get nine women in a room, they can produce a baby in a month."[108]

---

108 This interviewee wished to remain anonymous, but I can mention that they work for a sampling marketplace company.

It is hard enough to understand the nuances and limitations of a single panel. It is darn near impossible to understand the limitations of a sample when using a marketplace that cobbles together respondents from dozens of sources. I have no idea where the people who answer my surveys come from when I use a sample marketplace.

The highest quality sample providers do not contribute their most validated panelists to the marketplaces. They do not need to, as they can reserve their best poll takers for their own work.

Consequently, the best sample providers use these marketplaces as a place to dump their spare capacity. They make their poorest quality inventory available to the marketplaces, hoping that a researcher will buy them.

The marketplaces become like Craigslist for survey researchers. There may be high-quality things available on Craigslist, but you are never sure if you can trust what you are getting. It is often easier to go straight to the source and buy.

Nonetheless, sample marketplaces have become popular ways to source respondents for pollsters. The trend in polling is to do things fast and cheap, without much concern for quality.

CHAPTER 9

DATA COLLECTION ERRORS AND OMISSIONS

NOBODY SCOLDS US WHEN WE WRITE
A BAD QUESTION ANYMORE

Online opinion polls are not as well written as telephone polls were 20–30 years ago. I chalk this up to a lack of direct contact between survey authors and respondents.

Most data collection was via telephone when I started in survey research. A telephone call center was attached to our building. I would write a questionnaire, and on the first evening of the study, I would brief interviewers on the survey and get on the phone myself to conduct a few interviews. I would spend the next couple of hours listening in on other interviews.

There would be a debriefing session with interviewers at the night's end. Interviewers were not shy about telling me when my question wording was poor. They would tell me where people misunderstood what I was asking and what was not working. Failing to do my job well made their job awkward.

The next day, I would revise the questionnaire using their feedback. The following evening, the process would repeat.

The result was excellent questionnaires because I learned from interviewers and the people who answered my polls. I could tell what was and was not working in a way that is not possible by looking at data.

Now the questionnaires I write are for online surveys. There is no analogous feedback mechanism. On large studies, a client will have the time and budget for a proper pretest to talk to respondents about the questioning, but this is done on maybe 5% of market research projects and not on a single pre-election poll.

The result is online survey experiences that can be awkward and tortuous. We have lost our connection to the people who answer the questions we pose.

Errors during study fielding are rarely brought up as root causes of poor polling. Methodologists and upper-level project staff who critique the polls are not involved in day-to-day project management. They do not appreciate the complexity of study fielding. They can be oblivious to the errors that arise along the way.

THE ELEPHANT IN THE RESEARCH ROOM (NONRESPONSE BIAS)

If I had to pin polling's problems on one cause, it would be the (lack of) response to polls, stemming from the public's lack of interest in the polls and lack of trust in pollsters. Nonresponse bias is not just the elephant in the room. It is a herd of elephants in a tiny space.

The ability to project from a well-drawn sample is an underappreciated human discovery. It has led to improvements in our quality of life. Impressed at how quickly medical researchers developed the COVID-19 vaccines? You can, in part, thank the discovery of the statistical techniques that allow researchers to project vaccine efficacy by testing them on a sample of people in a clinical trial. Random projectible samples are one of humankind's greatest under-the-radar inventions.

This elegant invention assumes one of two things in polling. Either (1) everybody the researcher attempts to interview responds, or (2) those who choose not to respond would have answered the survey the same way as those who do.

If assumption #1 was true, there might not be any worries about the accuracy of pre-election polls. Pre-election polls would be accurate if every person contacted took part and answered honestly. That may be an unachievable ideal, but pollsters have done little to work toward it.

Since #1 is never true on a survey, researchers go ahead and assume that #2 is true. Ignoring nonresponse bias was a sensible assumption in the early days of market research and polling when most people would respond. It is no longer wise because so few people choose to answer our polls.

SURVEY RESPONSE RATES ARE SHOCKINGLY LOW

Today's political polls garner pathetic response rates. People are polarized in their opinions. Opinion polling violates the second assumption, which is likely a primary reason polls miss the mark.

In the late '80s/early '90s, we had a spreadsheet program to estimate project cost. One parameter in this spreadsheet was "refusal rate"—the percentage of people who would decline to participate in a study. The higher the estimated refusal rate, the more time and effort it would take to find people willing to complete the survey, and consequently, the more the study would cost.

Although the refusal rate varied by study, the base case assumption in this program was 40%. Researchers could expect that 60% of people contacted would cooperate. Rob Santos at the *Los Angeles Times* wrote:

> Thirty years ago, polling in the United States was simple. Most homes had land-line telephones, most people at home actually answered the phone and more than 70% were willing to participate. Polling life was sweet; it was easy to find a representative sample of likely voters.[109]

My first employer[110] (in 1989) was a local pollster who was quickly building a national reputation and was well known in the area where I lived. We conducted a lot of local polls. I remember being at social gatherings, and when I would tell people where I worked, they would either talk about how fun it was to take a poll we had called them for or complain that we had never called them.

Back then, people wanted to participate in polls and be heard.

---

109 Rob Santos, "Op-Ed: Why the Polls Get It Wrong,'" *Los Angeles Times*, March 27, 2016, https://www.latimes.com/opinion/op-ed/la-oe-0327-santos-polling-problems-20160327-story.html.

110 The Gordon S. Black Corporation, which became Harris Interactive after a series of acquisitions. This firm had about 30 employees when I joined in 1989 and about 1,000 when I left in 2006.

Now there are so many outlets for expressing opinions that polls are seen as an annoyance.

According to Pew and AAPOR, in 2018, the cooperation rate for telephone surveys was 6% and falling rapidly.[111] That means one in 17 people contacted agreed to participate in a telephone survey. From 1990 until now, we have gone from one in 1.7 people willing to take part to one in 17 people willing to take part—a response rate that is 10 times worse than it used to be.[112]

Online survey cooperation rates are hard to calculate in a standardized way. Most estimates I have seen suggest that typical online cooperation rates are less than 5%. For a 1,000-person survey, researchers send between 30,000 and 40,000 invitations, as they also have to account for the bad quality respondents they will get.

To put it another way, to get an audience the size of what the Beacon Theatre in New York City holds to answer a survey, you would likely have to send out invitations to an audience the size of MetLife Stadium's capacity.[113]

Many factors have led to this response decline. People have become less trusting of institutions, including pollsters. They are more distracted, and technologies used to poll them are avenues to this distraction. They have more venues to vent their

---

111 Kennedy and Hartig, "Response Rates in Telephone Surveys Have Resumed Their Decline."

112 AAPOR developed standards on how telephone research response rates are calculated. They are available at https://www.aapor.org/Education-Resources/For-Researchers/Poll-Survey-FAQ/Response-Rates-An-Overview.aspx. There is no analog for the calculation of online response rates.

113 The Beacon Theatre's capacity is 2,894; MetLife Stadium's capacity is 82,500.

opinions beyond the polls. CBS News' Elections and Surveys Director Anthony Salvanto wrote:

> People today are also more immune to that old pollster's appeal to "make your voice heard" by taking a poll. There are a lot of outlets for expressing your view now; even if they aren't scientific they can feel more instantaneous.[114]

Poor response rates are not the problem per se. The problem is a lack of representativeness. In theory, a dataset with a low response rate could be representative, while one with a high response rate could have a large bias. Researchers grab onto this concept and try to convince clients that response rates do not matter. They do.

The two concepts are related—nonresponse bias grows as response rates drop.[115] Most observers would agree that having one in 17 people complete a poll is not good for data quality.

Low response rates are responsible for botched polling predictions. As Robert Groves, a former Census Bureau director points out:

> The risk of failures of surveys to reflect the facts increases with falling response rates. The risk is not always realized, but with the very low response rates now common, we should expect more failed predictions based on surveys.[116]

---

114 Salvanto, *Where Did You Get This Number?*

115 Robert M. Groves, Floyd J. Fowler Jr., Mick P. Couper, James M. Lepkowski, Eleanor Singer, and Roger Tourangeau, *Survey Methodology* (Hoboken, NJ: Wiley, 2011).

116 Ibid.

According to one research executive:

> Non-response bias is potentially huge. Here's a technically correct statement (that we did not see) for a poll with a 5% response rate: Our poll indicates Biden will achieve 50% of the vote, +/–48 points after we take into account theoretical non-response error.[117]

This degree of error is what Humphrey Taylor implied when he mused that the potential for error is infinite.

Market researchers do not like to discuss response rates. We hope clients will not ask the question. Panel companies and research agencies obfuscate if you ask them about response rates. If you are a market research client and want to have fun, ask your research agency what the response rate was on your project and listen to them dance around the topic. You quickly learn that they do not want to disclose your response rate or do not know what it is.

Let us be clear on what the problem is. For an online pre-election poll of 1,000 people, pollsters have to send about 35,000 invitations to complete the study. Thirty-four thousand of the people emailed will not respond at all or not in a way that allows their data to be confidently placed in the database.

When calculating who is ahead in the election, the pollster assumes that the 34,000 people who did not respond would express the same candidate preferences as the 1,000 who did. This is a tenuous assumption.

---

117 Author interview with George Terhanian.

Nonresponse is not random. Certain age groups (young people, older people), men, minorities, and rural populations are less apt to answer surveys than others. Those who spend more time online and have technology more at the center of their lives respond at greater rates to online surveys. Politically active people are more likely to respond.

These groups likely have different views on the day's issues and different voter preferences than their counterparts. Nonresponse bias is a bias that matters.

Methodologists do what they can to address this through quota sampling and weighting. It is easy enough to ensure a reasonable age distribution and equal numbers of men and women are interviewed. This helps.

Nonresponse issues exist within these groups. Men who choose to respond might not be representative of all male voters. The older folks who answer might not be like those who choose not to respond.

No amount of quota sampling or weighting can address this problem. Methodologists try, but it is not possible to weight your way out of the issues caused by nonresponse.

This problem is correctable in theory. Researchers can do a sampling of nonresponders. The data needed to fix the problem can be gathered if researchers randomly sample those who did not respond initially.

In 30 years of conducting survey research studies, I can recall only one project where the client sampled nonresponders. That study was for an academic researcher, and their grant application required them to do so. It took six months and specially trained interviewers to do it. We vowed never to commit to a project like this again because of the time and expense required.

All other pre-election polling issues are inconsequential compared to nonresponse bias. If everyone contacted for surveys agreed to take part, polls would be predictive and trusted.

As George Terhanian stated in the Foreword to this book, the firm we worked for (Harris Interactive) made 72 forecasts for the 2000 election. These predictions covered the presidential race both nationally and in 38 states and key statewide contests for the Senate and governorships.

Harris' 2000 online polls correctly predicted 70 of these 72 races and came closer to predicting the presidential popular vote than any national phone polls.

When they were released, these polls were strongly derided by other pollsters because the Harris polls were conducted online when only about 52% of Americans had broadband access.

This begs a question. How did online pre-election polls succeed in 2000 if only half of the population had broadband access when online polls largely failed in 2020 when over 90% had access?[118] Did Harris get lucky?

The answer is no. The core reason the 2000 online polls succeeded where the 2020 polls failed is that response rates were

---

118   "Internet/Broadband Factsheet," Pew Research Center, April 7, 2021, https://www.pewresearch.org/internet/fact-sheet/internet-broadband/.

high, and response biases were low. Harris was able to accurately represent the 52% of the population that was online in 2000 and calibrate this to the larger population of voters. Harris used a parallel telephone poll (which also had a high response) to thoroughly understand the differences between voters who had online access versus those who did not.

The method[119] is sophisticated and was new to the polling field. It worked because response rates were high, which provided reliable data.

Harris' 2000 success underscores how innovative methodologists can do amazing things—if they have good data.

Recent polls (from about 2012 onward) have missed the mark because polling methodologists *do not* have good data. The response rates to polls are under 5% and dropping rapidly. The resulting response biases are so severe that even the most talented statisticians cannot work miracles with the data. The tools pollsters used in the past no longer work.

The problem is the polling field has not recognized this. Pollsters expect methodologists to pull a rabbit out of a hat because they have done so in the past. But a researcher cannot "weight their way" out of a poor dataset. Even the best chef in the world cannot make a filet out of hamburger.

---

119 The method used is called propensity score matching.

DID YOU KNOW POLLSTERS IGNORE AT LEAST A THIRD OF THE PEOPLE WHO ANSWER THEIR SURVEYS?

Poor-quality data is an increasing problem for researchers. Currently, between a third and half of people who respond merit exclusion from our collected survey data.

There are many causes of poor-quality respondents. Survey designers show little empathy for those who take their surveys. Researchers torture them with poorly worded or irrelevant questions and lengthy surveys. They pay piddling incentives and fail to thank or respect people for their cooperation.

This lack of respect for people results from the evolution from telephone interviewing to online data collection. In a telephone survey, an interviewer establishes a relationship. A human voice thanks a person for taking part. People feel appreciated. The survey experience is a social one.

In contrast, online interviewing is faceless and often heartless. As researchers, we have made it that way.

When designing phone studies, I was respectful that I needed to interrupt 1,000 people having dinner to complete my poll. I would hear what was going on in the background of their lives. I wanted this interruption to be worth it to them. When reviewing our poll questions, my boss and I would ask each other, "Is this worth interrupting dinner to ask?"

Online, a few buttons are pressed, and data magically appear. The process is dehumanized.

People today are distracted while taking polls in a way they were not before. Many people take polls on mobile devices while watching TV, socializing with friends, and so forth. It is difficult to get a person's undivided attention anymore.

We asked people if they were doing other things while taking our Crux Poll. Twenty-four percent were watching TV or a video. Twenty percent were eating. In total, almost half (48%) of our poll takers were doing a distracting activity when taking our poll.

Landline telephone studies tethered respondents to a specific environment. Online and cell phone studies introduce a new source of variability into a project: the context in which data are collected varies by the respondent.

Online polls are subject to the internet's dark side. Survey bots filling out online questionnaires are so prevalent that firms have arisen to protect against them. On every project we do, we find many open-ended (typed) responses obviously written by an AI program and not a human.

Imperium is a company that helps combat poor-quality respondents. They state that the trend toward poor quality picked up in pace in 2020:

> In spring this year we identified a 25 percent increase in fraudulent survey respondents; more recently we have seen this spiking to around double the expected numbers. And, while we're witnessing an inevitable rise in fraudsters trying to enter surveys, even verified respondents are providing less actionable insights.[120]

---

120 Tim McCarthy, "Prioritizing Quality: Tackling the COVID-19 Spike in Survey Fraud Head-on," Imperium, 2020, https://www.imperium.com/2020/11/24/prioritizing-quality-tackling-the-covid-19-spike-in-survey-fraud-head-on/.

Researchers guard against bad-quality respondents. Sampling companies do what they can to keep them out of their databases, with many kicked out before they ever get to the survey. Yet, plenty get through.

Ever speed your way through a survey? Well, if you completed it too quickly, your answers were likely voided. Researchers will remove your data if you give inconsistent responses, type gibberish into an open-ended question, or select the same answer too many times in a row. Do this on more than one survey, and researchers will no longer reach out.

There is no industry standard for removing bad-quality respondents, which makes it a source of variability across polls from different polling organizations. Some researchers are more aggressive than others in tossing respondents. Most are not bold enough because it is expensive to throw data away.

Rather than automated ways of removing respondents, the most effective method is a subjective, manual process. Research assistants flag respondents who need to be looked at further. A staff member painstakingly looks through answers and decides whether this person is worthy of inclusion. Each pollster has its own rules on which people should stay and which should be removed. It is a bit of a mess, as one reviewer might toss a respondent while another might keep them in the database.

This laborious process is hard to do for 1,000 respondents in a day or two. Pollsters skip this quality check when polls field too quickly, letting more poor-quality respondents get through than with polls fielded across a more extended period.

The result is problems on both ends: researchers can get it wrong by leaving bad-quality respondents in the database and by being too aggressive and removing good-quality respondents.

In the best scenario, included poor-quality respondents cause random errors and do not affect results. In this case, they effectively lower the sample size and the poll's precision. If poor-quality respondents do not answer randomly, they can considerably affect the poll's results.

This problem cannot be overstated. If a pollster does nothing to correct for bad respondents, between a third and half of their data will be bogus. Good pollsters discover and remove these respondents. Most are leaving too many bad respondents in their databases.

In the Crux Poll we created for this book, we fielded over 11 days to have adequate time to catch bad respondents. We removed 25% of respondents for quality control reasons, and we suspect that just like pollsters, we failed to remove enough. Just three years ago, we removed only 10% of our respondents for quality control.

This problem is massive. It is an existential threat to the survey research and polling fields.

Like other issues, the industry's reaction is to fight it with science—by coming up with complicated programs and sampling methods, rather than establishing a greater degree of trust between researchers and respondents, which would get at the core cause of the problem.

DIY TOOLS ALLOW BAD RESEARCHERS TO
DO THEIR OWN BAD RESEARCH

Over the past decade, a market research innovation has occurred that is talked about in hushed tones among research agencies: the rise of do-it-yourself (DIY) market research tools. Researchers and clients need to become more educated about these DIY tools and when to use them.

DIY tools come in several flavors. They allow anybody to log into a system, author a survey, select sample parameters, and hit "go." Many also provide the ability to tabulate data and graph results. These tools reduce the complexity of fielding studies.

Many research agencies view DIY tools as an existential threat. After all, if clients can do all this, why do they need us? Will our fielding and programming departments become obsolete? Will a large part of what we do become automated?

Maybe. But more likely, our fielding and programming departments will become smaller and adapt to a changing technological world.

There is a clear analogy to DIY household projects. Tools and materials needed for home improvement projects are available at big-box retailers. Some homeowners are well equipped to take on projects while others are not. The key to a successful project is understanding when to call for professional help. The same is true for market research projects.

The analogy fails when a client takes on a project they are not equipped to handle. If it is a home project, you may realize you are in over your head and call a professional.

In market research and polling, you can complete an entire project with serious errors and never notice. The project will result in suboptimal decision making, and nobody may notice.

In days gone by, whether to use a research agency or not was straightforward. If the project was meaningful or complex, clients used agencies. For many projects, the choice used to be between using an agency or not doing the project.

The rise of DIY tools has changed that. DIY studies have their place. That place is not in pre-election or opinion polling. Pre-election polling needs to be precise, and minor errors can make the difference between a successful and unsuccessful prediction.

Currently, some poorly funded pollsters use DIY tools for their pre-election polls, but these tools are used primarily for opinion polling. The use of DIY tools results from financial pressures: polling is challenging to make money on, pollsters are forced to find ways to cut costs, and DIY polls are one way to do so.

WE CHANGE PEOPLE BY SURVEYING THEM

A concept in physics is known as the observer effect. It means that the very act of trying to observe or measure can disturb or change the subject. Trying to measure an object distorts it.

Quantum mechanics aside, this problem exists in market research and polling. A clear scenario is when researchers try to measure an opinion that does not exist.

I am not kidding when I say that I once had a client compel me to put a question like this into a study: "How would you rate the mouth-feel of the last 16-ounce bottle of water you bought at a convenience store?"

Asking a question like this literally changes the person we are interviewing. Researchers are seeking an unformed opinion. In the 10 seconds allotted to answer the question, a person's brain must form new connections to answer.

Have you ever thought of what the "mouth-feel" of the last bottle of water you drank was? Do you even know what "mouth-feel" is?

I have forged new connections in your brain by asking you to consider this question. I have physically changed you.

Changing consumers' minds is the goal of marketers. It is not the goal of market researchers and pollsters. Researchers should aim to observe unobtrusively.

Observer effects happen on political opinion polls. Pollsters ask nuanced questions because they want to understand details. People may not think about issues in the level of detail pollsters want. When we ask questions, we get answers.

I am sure I got statistics related to bottled water's "mouth-feel," just as opinion pollsters get answers to detailed questions. This does not mean the answers are meaningful.

The observer effect is likely small on pre-election polls. Most voters have considered whom they will vote for before the survey takes place. It seems unlikely that taking part in a pre-election poll could sway voting behavior.

Yet, the observer effect begets a more relevant problem known as a panel learning effect. The act of asking for an opinion can affect someone's future behavior. This learning effect causes them to become less representative.

Pollsters need to take care not to survey the same person twice. When researchers measure advertising awareness, previously interviewed people are no longer representative because they learned about the advertising campaign during the original survey. Measuring their opinions on a survey caused them to become more likely to notice the ads in the future.

In the same way, taking part in a political poll may cause a person to have conversations with others they might not otherwise have had. It can influence them to pay more attention to the news. The act of measuring your preferences changes you.

Many pre-election polls fail to exclude previous respondents. Even pollsters that exclude prior respondents cannot control for all the other polls that are going on that might have interviewed the same individual. There is cross-pollination between sample sources—some of the same people are in different panels and answer polls in other ways. Most pollsters are getting their respondents from the same two or three companies.

Online panels are filled with "professional poll takers." When conducting random digit dialing (RDD) telephone samples, it is common to reach people who have never answered a poll before or who have done so only a handful of times in their lifetimes. When using online panels, it is normal to reach people who take dozens of polls annually.

We asked about this in the Crux Poll. This online poll utilized the same sample provider[121] used by many top pollsters. On average, those who answered the Crux Poll had responded to four surveys or polls in the past month. That is 48 polls per year on average.[122] That is 48 chances for a poll to change the respondent.

The resulting panel learning bias may not matter to many studies. I have looked at research data to see if the number of polls a person takes affects response and rarely find anything consequential. Pre-election polls may be different, and this issue has gone unstudied by the research community and political scientists.

CAN ONLINE POLLS GET IT RIGHT?

Survey research has transitioned from live interviewer (telephone) data collection to online data collection. Pre-election polls are an exception—it is the one form of survey research that still significantly uses telephone research. Some pollsters still do not feel that online polling can provide reasonable estimates.

In the broader field of market research, telephone data collection has been relegated to studies with large budgets that seek a difficult-to-reach respondent base. Researchers try not to propose telephone data collection because of cost.

Plenty of research exists on the pros and cons of online polling. Most academic papers take two to four years from data

---

121   www.dynata.com.

122   In the Crux Poll, the number of polls a person responded to did not correlate strongly with how much or little they trusted pollsters.

collection to publication. As internet penetration has grown, the nature of what people are doing online and their time with devices has evolved. Although the academic inquiries are informative, they tend to be outdated. The digital world changes by the time these studies are published. For this reason, it is not possible to definitively say whether telephone or online polls are better, if only because what is meant by "online poll" changes by the time academics make this judgment.

The jury is still out on whether online or telephone polls provide better popular vote estimates. The two forms of data collection get similar results, and there are likely not enough polls of each type to make a definitive assessment of which method is better and why.

CAN TELEPHONE POLLS GET IT RIGHT?

Telephone polls used to be able to get it right. From the 1950s through the 1970s, most American households had one landline, and most telephone numbers were available in listed directories. RDD could reach those who chose not to list their numbers. Telephone companies assigned phone numbers in a way that allowed pollsters to know where they were calling based on the phone number's area code and exchange. Response rates were high.

Since that time, technological changes that have occurred in telephony has served to make polling more difficult:

- People started using more than one landline.
- Technologies such as answering machines and caller ID devices allowed people to prescreen their calls. Many chose to stop answering calls from pollsters.

- The Do Not Call Registry caused survey response rates to plummet.[123]
- Cell phones arose, with no national directory of cell numbers. Cell numbers were not assigned geographically, beyond their area codes, which resulted in challenges for researchers and pollsters to geo-target their calls.
- Phone numbers became portable. If a person moved from one state to another, they could fail to be included in the sampling frame in their new state because researchers could not determine where they lived from their phone number.
- The launch of the first smartphone (the iPhone) in 2007 ushered in an era where most Americans own a piece of technology that has become the favored device to use when responding to surveys. Although mobile surveys are user friendly, they also maximize distractions. They do not allow the researcher to control the interview's context.
- 4G networks made it practical for cell phones to stream video and use the internet, thus ensuring many people would be increasingly distracted when answering surveys.
- Apple placed a new feature on the iPhone that automatically routes unknown callers to voicemail.[124] This feature was quickly copied on Android phones and made getting a good telephone sample for opinion surveys even harder.

As the chart below shows, landline telephone penetration grew slowly and steadily across the 20th century and peaked in 1999. It took 75 years for landline phones to go from 10% to above 90% in household penetration.

---

123 The Do Not Call Registry does not prohibit polls, but it still caused many people to stop answering them.

124 "A New iPhone Feature Poses a Threat to Opinion Pollsters," *The Economist*, September 26, 2019, https://www.economist.com/united-states/2019/09/26/a-new-iphone-feature-poses-a-threat-to-opinion-pollsters.

In contrast, cell phones took 15 years to make the same leap. In about 2003, more households had access to a cell phone than a landline.

Share of US Households Using Specific Technologies (1903 to 2019)

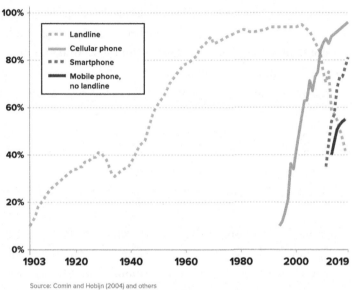

Source: Comin and Hobijn (2004) and others
OurWorldInData.org/technology-adoption

This chart shows we are approaching a time when 60% of US households do not have landlines and are "cell phone only." It has become methodologically impossible to conduct a project-ible poll solely using landlines. The polling field has been slow to adapt and still has not found a viable way around this problem.

Telephone research (using RDD samples) had a 25-year heyday from the middle of the 1970s until the turn of the century. This resulted in heavy investments in telephone research centers and telephony. These investments caused many research firms to be slow to adapt to a new world of mobile phones and online data collection. The high legacy costs of these investments continue to have a lasting effect on the quality of polling.

Plummeting response rates[125] made telephone polls untenable. It costs 10 times more to conduct a telephone study today than 20 years ago. Telephone polling is the only product or service I can think of that has increased in price more than a college education and healthcare.

Although pre-election poll injuries seem self-inflicted, the increasing mismatch of telephone (and online) sampling frames to the voter population is a genuine threat to the polling industry. A pollster can do everything else right, but the poll is doomed if they fail to talk to the right people.

---

125   According to the Pew Research Center, telephone response rates were 36% in 1997 and fell to 6% in 2018.

CHAPTER 10

THE POLLSTERS' SECRET SAUCE HAS TURNED BAD

ON SURVEYS, PEOPLE OVERSTATE WHAT THEY WILL DO IN THE FUTURE

I remember the first time I worked on a market research project and discovered people were overly optimistic in saying what they would do.

A city hired the firm I worked for to determine if it was feasible to seek an expansion NHL franchise. This city was in a hockey hotbed. It had a successful minor league team and a fantastic new arena. A professional hockey team seemed like a good fit.

We surveyed the population that lived within about an hour's drive from the arena. We showed people ticket prices and asked how many games they would attend if the NHL gave this city a franchise.

I was an inexperienced researcher (and a hockey fan) a year out of business school at the time. I got the first crack at this data. I multiplied the percentage of people who indicated they would attend by how many tickets they said they would buy. I projected this up to the population for the area. I took these numbers into our research VP, who was excited because this showed enthusiastic support for the team.

He gave me a high five. We were going to help this city get an NHL team!

I thought about this projection more when I returned to my office. I divided it by the number of seats in the arena multiplied by the number of home games. I realized the number I came up with meant 16 people would occupy each seat in the arena for each game!

I reviewed NHL attendance statistics and discovered not a single franchise had sold out all seats for all games in the previous season. We had grossly overestimated the potential attendance.

I returned to the research VP. We reviewed everything on the study: its sampling, the question wording, my calculations, and so forth. We showed our calculations to other researchers not involved in the project to see if they could spot an error. We had not made any obvious mistakes.

I remain convinced we did not do anything technically wrong on the project, yet the projections were off.

The problem? We failed to have a way to compensate for the difference between what people say they will do and what they will do.[126]

Election pollsters face a similar problem: people vastly overstate their likelihood of voting. Pollsters deal with this problem in different ways—which is a primary reason why two polls using almost identical methods can yield different predictions.

---

126 This city did not end up getting an NHL franchise despite our optimistic projections.

This is the second biggest cause of polling misses (after low response rates)—predicting who will show up to vote has proved challenging for pollsters.

Methodologists focus on sampling errors when looking for causes of polls that miss the mark. Yet, errors after the data collection stage are as consequential as sampling errors.

HERDING—POLLSTERS ARE AFRAID TO LOOK DIFFERENT

It sounds trite, but polls should follow the laws of statistics. When multiple polls are released in a similar time frame, their predictions should normally distribute (like a bell curve). Predictions of vote percentage should converge around an average measure, and the spread of the distribution should behave predictably.[127]

Specifically, about two-thirds of polls should be within one standard deviation of the average, and about 95% should be within two. This is a basic statistical concept.

This might sound complicated, but it can be simplified: when the results of all the polls are plotted on a graph, math tells us what the shape of this graph should be (a bell). We should suspect something is amiss when this graph does not have a bell shape.

There is a tendency to think that if all the polls are reporting similar results, we can be confident regarding what will happen in the election. It more likely means something might be wrong.

---

127 This is known as the standard normal, or Z distribution.

The media should worry if they do *not* see an occasional poll from a reputable pollster that seems off.

A lack of variability in poll findings is evidence of a problem known as *herding*. Herding is a tendency for pollsters to suppress results that differ from what other polls are reporting. If reputable pollsters say a candidate has a five-point lead and my poll says they have a 10-point lead, I have to be gutsy to put my poll out there for public scrutiny.

Pollsters are like teenagers. They want to stand out, but at the same time, they are afraid of being seen as "too different" by their peers.

This mentality causes some polls to be buried and not released. It causes others to be released after the data have been adjusted to look like everyone else's polls.

AAPOR recognizes herding as a problem:

> With multiple pollsters releasing results on the same basic questions at about the same time, political pollsters want to avoid being seen as the one firm that got it wrong. To avoid raising questions regarding the accuracy of their results, some political pollsters adjust their findings to match or closely approximate the results of other polls.[128]

When a poll looks like it may not conform, this causes pollsters to review and tweak their likely voter models, their weighting formulae, and so forth. Nonconforming polls receive more

---

128 "Herding," American Association of Public Opinion Research, accessed February 15, 2022, https://www.aapor.org/Education-Resources/Election-Polling-Resources/Herding.aspx.

internal scrutiny by methodologists than polls that support what other pollsters are showing. The result is polls that all look about the same.

A perfectly executed poll can be far off an election result. This is expected—one in 20 polls should be more than two standard deviations away from the result.

It is disastrous for a pollster to publish a poll like this. A pollster can be right and wrong at the same time. A perfect poll can be released and harm the pollster's reputation.

Herding in polls can be consequential for candidates. In 2016 and 2020, polling influenced which candidates were allowed on the primary debate stages. Herding artificially suppresses variation in poll results, causing the media and the candidates to think public opinion is more uniform than it likely is. Polling data in 2016 and 2020 showed more certainty around who merited inclusion on the debate stages than was the case because of herding.

Pollsters denounce herding, yet they all do it. They may not suppress a poll, but they scrutinize those that fail to conform to expectations and tweak their models. Herding is a tragedy-of-the-commons problem—by behaving in their self-interest, pollsters make themselves look better but make the overall polling industry look worse.

Nate Silver at FiveThirtyEight has written an article[129] that

129 Nate Silver, "Here's Proof Some Pollsters Are Putting a Thumb on the Scale,"
     FiveThirtyEight, November 14, 2014, https://fivethirtyeight.com/features/
     heres-proof-some-pollsters-are-putting-a-thumb-on-the-scale/.

shows herding behavior among pollsters increases later in an election cycle. That makes sense—as more polls are published, there is more of a target to herd toward and a greater consequence to pollsters if their predictions are wrong.

We can see herding happening, but it is impossible to tell who is doing it. We can see it happening when poll results across pollsters do not vary much. Since herded polls fail to get published, we do not know who the violators are.

HOUSE EFFECTS—NOT ALL RESEARCHERS ARE NEUTRAL

A "house effect" is a bias.[130] It is a tendency for a specific pollster to have results that consistently skew in a direction that supports conservative or liberal candidates. It should not be present at all as data should be neutral.

With notable exceptions, pollsters want to be viewed as politically neutral. It does not help their research business for their polls to favor either side.

House effects show how polling is a human business, as they are present even among reputable pollsters. They tend to be unintentional and subtle among the best-known pollsters. Perhaps emboldened by the business success of partisan media outlets, the new maverick pollsters are not scared to reveal their political leanings.

House effects are not about a single poll, which might be off in

---

130 A house "effect" is how a pollster's data tends to skew in relation to other pollsters. A house "bias" is how a pollster's data tends to skew in relation to election results.

any direction. They refer more to tendencies—a pollster might be regularly off in one direction or the other.

Thankfully, house biases tend to be small—the bulk are less than +/-1%. They vary over time as well and can be surprising. For instance, would you have guessed the house bias for Fox News' polls would be favorable for Biden over Trump in 2020? It was.

There are as many house biases toward the conservative side as toward the liberal side. Although they are a potential problem for any individual pollster, they are an unlikely culprit for what ails the polls overall.

THE POLLSTERS' SECRET—THE LIKELY VOTER MODEL

Too much subjectivity is involved in predicting voter turnout. I conducted a poll relating to a medium-sized city's mayoral race in 1993. Our poll had the Democratic candidate, who had never run for public office, winning by 10%.

The day before the election, I showed the results to my boss. He was scheduled to be on a local television station on election night to present our poll and discuss the election results.

He quickly scanned the data from our pre-election poll. He told me the data had to be reweighted because it was clear the Democratic candidate would win in a landslide. He was correct, as this candidate won the election with 72% of the vote.

He did not make this assertion from a political position or out of hope. We had completed a poll of area residents who were registered and likely to vote and had a high response rate. When he perused the data, he noticed that the demographic categories of voters that were likely to turn out in an off-year local election favored this candidate.

He knew the poll, which seemed methodologically sound, was seriously off in its prediction.

His experience as a pollster and political scientist helped him determine who would show up. He was correct, but his approach was not scientific.

That was when I learned pre-election polling is as much of an art as a science. I was uncomfortable. We seemed to be putting our foot on the scale as we reweighted the poll to conform to the gut feel of our expert.

What today's pollsters do is as subjective as what my boss did. The difference is they veil this subjectivity in complicated statistics. They let methodologists develop a statistical model that predicts the chance you will vote. Many of their choices in developing these models are subjective.

Pre-election polls are among the most straightforward types of projects researchers do. Yet, a feature of pre-election polls complicates them. This element makes or breaks a pre-election poll: its likely voter model (LVM).

An LVM seeks to adjust for the fact that many more people *say* they are eligible to and will vote than *actually do so*. An LVM is what pollsters use to determine the likelihood that someone who *says* they will vote will.

Even in the high-turnout 2020 election, where about two-thirds of the adult US population voted, about 90% of polling respondents said they would show up.

The poll takers are not lying. They expect to show up to vote. But some forget to do so. Their cars do not start, their life obligations do not allow them to get there in time, and so on. Since the beginning of polling, more people have claimed they will vote than actually do so.

Woody Allen once remarked, "Eighty percent of success is showing up." For pollsters, 80% of their success is *predicting* who will show up. Beyond poor response rates, inaccurate LVMs are a major cause of polling misses.

It is easy to pose the right questions on a pre-election poll. Pollsters tend to interview the right mix of people. They are not so good at figuring out if the people taking their polls will show up on Election Day.

Predicting voter turnout is difficult. Pollsters are projecting to an unknown population (those who will vote) with unknown characteristics. The characteristics of the voting populace change with each election and are not known beforehand. Predicting who will turn out is a shot in the dark.

How do pollsters predict if you will vote? They rely on their experts. These experts determine your likelihood of voting by other things known about you. You get profiled.

Ironically, when researchers turn to research *scientists*, pre-election polling becomes art and not science.

The development of an LVM allows methodologists to move from their left (rational) brains to their right (creative) brains. If you have ever gotten to know a methodologist, you will agree that creativity is not their strong suit.

LIKELY VOTER MODELS ARE SUBJECTIVE

In 2016, Nate Cohn from *The New York Times* ran an experiment. He provided four reputable pollsters with the raw data from a presidential pre-election poll in Florida. Each pollster applied their proprietary LVM.

The outcome was a five-point spread in their calculations. The results ranged from one pollster having Trump leading by one point to another having Clinton leading by four points. Four experts, four different LVMs, four different answers from identical inputs.

Clearly, the reported margin of error due to sampling, even when including a design effect (which purports to capture the added uncertainty of weighting), doesn't even come close to capturing total survey error.[131]

This experiment shows that polling misfires are caused as much by what pollsters do with data as by how they collect it.

Most pollsters get their respondents from the same online and telephone sampling companies. The question for a horse-race poll is pretty much the same no matter which pollster poses it.

---

131 Nate Cohn, "We Gave Four Good Pollsters the Same Raw Data. They Had Four Different Results," *The New York Times*, September 20, 2016, https://www.nytimes.com/interactive/2016/09/20/upshot/the-error-the-polling-world-rarely-talks-about.html.

Even the survey software used to collect data is the same across most pollsters.

The result: presidential horse-race raw data is likely the same (among reputable pollsters) regardless of who conducted the poll. It is what the pollsters do with this data that is different and mysterious.

Pollsters regularly meet after presidential election cycles. They debate whether their models included too many Democrats or Republicans, if they had too many or too few minorities in their samples, and so forth.

The subjectivity inherent in the process is on full display in these meetings. Methodologists speculate about who will turn out to vote when they create predictions. These guesses are why reputable pollsters can make different conclusions from the same data.

Many methodologists fall into a classic "if all you have is a hammer, every problem looks like a nail" mindset. Top methodologists are more like academics than they are like marketers. Like academics, they have intense yet narrow expertise. As a result, their modeling is limited to this narrow expertise, which may have been honed years ago when they got their PhD.

Their fundamental mistake is to create voter turnout models based on past data. Methodologists fail to see broader, faster-moving things that are relevant to predicting if someone will vote.

An LVM is a "black box"—pollsters are notorious for not

disclosing what is in the model. It is like the formula for Coca-Cola—we can likely guess what the main ingredients are, but we do not know how they put them together or if they added something unexpected into the mix. LVMs are the trade secrets of pollsters.

A "model" can sound more complex than it is. A pollster is trying to discover if someone will vote based on what they know about them. Do you say you will vote? With how much certainty? Did you vote in the last election? What is your age? Your race? How strongly do you support your candidate?

These characteristics can help predict if you will show up.

These measures are placed in a regression model. This model allows a methodologist to guess the probability you will show up and vote. Each person is assigned a probability between 0% and 100% as a weighting factor. If you answer a poll and we determine your voting probability is 50%, you get half a vote in our tally.

There is an inherent problem in this. Nobody casts half of a vote. In the end, you either vote or not. Assigning probabilities to people proves wrong in all cases because these probabilities move to either 0% or 100% on Election Day.

Pollsters may address this by using a "cutoff model." A cutoff model picks a point, say 50%. Pollsters assume you will vote if an LVM puts you above 50%. If it is below 50%, they assume you will not.

The problem with a cutoff model approach is that it is subjective when applied. Why 50%? Why not 49% or 51%? The science behind determining the cutoff was derived using data from the previous election. What if the world has changed?

This process could be made less subjective by conducting studies after the election. Pollsters rarely recontact respondents to determine if they did show up to vote. That would enable them to calibrate their models for the next cycle.[132] New product researchers do this to calibrate—they resurvey people to see if they bought the product.

Pollsters rarely do this because nobody is paying them to do so. As I have stated, opinion polling is a terrible profession from a money standpoint. Pollsters did not pay for their nice cars from their polling work. Pollsters paid for these cars from their corporate market research projects.

A similar problem exists in new product research. Many more people say they will buy a new product than will. For our NHL project, I needed an LVM to predict if people would show up to the games. We assumed 100% of those who said they would go to a game would. The result was 16 people in each seat for every game. I needed a way to assess the probability that people would buy the tickets they indicated they would.

For new products, instead of voting probability, researchers want to know the likelihood someone will buy. Researchers look at variables such as the strength of interest in the product, past loyalty to the brand, dissatisfaction with existing similar products,

---

132 There is evidence that recontacting respondents after an election still overrepresents individuals who voted. This happened on the Crux Poll, where 80% of respondents indicated they had voted in the 2020 US presidential election. See Chi-lin Tsai, "A Re-examination of American National Election Studies to Resolve a Controversy about Who Overreports Turnout," *International Journal of Public Opinion Research* 32, no. 4 (2020): 780–89, https://doi.org/10.1093/ijpor/edaa011.

and so on to try to put a finer point on market projections. We ask about a current product with known sales to help calibrate.

We still overshoot the actual market size. It is a problem. I tell clients if they are happy with a market size that is one-third of what we tell them, they should go forth with the product launch.

Pre-election polling is no different—most LVMs overpredict voter turnout.

Some market research firms specialize in "volumetric forecasting." They create a regression model that uses variables such as marketing spending, projected effectiveness of advertising, expected product distribution and reach, pricing, competitive sales, and so forth as predictor variables. They sprinkle in findings from a research study on the new product's appeal. This model considers these variables and yields an estimate of how well the new product will sell.

This is sophisticated, and it works. These estimates predict sales of tens of millions of dollars within a 10% error band. (Clients pay dearly for them as well, as these studies are among the most expensive studies market researchers conduct.)

How does market research do such an effective job at projecting sales? Well, research firms calibrate these models. The firms specializing in this type of research have done thousands of these studies. They get a real-world assessment of how well their predictions were. They use these sales figures to continually tweak their models to enhance their predictiveness in the future.[133]

---

133 This modeling does not work well with certain products, especially innovative products that are creating new product categories. They are notoriously bad predictors of sales for technology products with little current frame of reference for the respondent.

Pre-election pollsters cannot do this because there are not thousands of elections to feed calibration. Pollsters do calibrate to past elections, but the data they use can go back decades and not be relevant to today's world.

Big data might come to the rescue. It is theoretically possible to link voter files to respondents. Privacy issues aside for a moment, your state does not know whom you voted for, but they do know if you voted. The US Census keeps a record of your detailed demographic information. Your state and federal income tax information exist. Google and Facebook track your online behavior.

For the first time, the computing power (and analytical muscle) exists to combine these datasets. This combined dataset may help refine LVMs. Researchers can use demographics and tax information to predict who will vote more accurately. This approach could be better than relying on polling information alone.

Serious data privacy issues are at play in this. It might not be possible for pollsters (who are private companies) to get this information. But academic researchers can.[134] These data might improve LVMs. The primary data problem with this approach arises because it takes academic researchers up to a decade to publish. They run the risk of predicting past elections but not future ones.

---

134 To see what a Harvard professor has done using data like what I describe, visit http://www.rajchetty.com/.

POLLSTERS NEED TO DISCLOSE MORE
ABOUT THEIR LIKELY VOTER MODELS

LVMs vary from pollster to pollster. Pollsters rarely discuss LVMs because they are trade secrets. Yet, LVMs are a leading contributor to the inaccuracy of pre-election polls.

Pollsters would be well served to disclose their LVM results—that is, their predictions for voter turnout. The reality is that LVMs overpredict voter turnout and misproject millions of votes.

Consider these hypothetical examples from 2020:

- Poll A predicts Biden will defeat Trump by eight points—54% to 46%. Its LVM predicts a 60% turnout.
- Poll B predicts Biden will beat Trump by four points—52% to 48%. Its LVM predicts an 80% turnout.

The election result was a 4.5-point Biden victory. Which poll was better, poll A or poll B?

When the polls' prediction for turnout is not considered, poll B is the better poll, as it came within 0.5 points of the actual vote margin, while poll A was off by 3.5 points. Most evaluators of pollsters would give poll B the better performance grade.

Yet, if we do the math and project how many votes each poll is predicting for each candidate, poll A comes out the winner.

	BIDEN	TRUMP	TURNOUT
ACTUAL RESULT	81,268,924	74,216,154	66%
POLL A	76,098,437	64,824,594	60%
POLL B	97,706,635	90,190,740	80%

Poll A underprojected Biden by 5,170,487 votes and Trump by 9,391,560 votes. So in total, it underprojected about 14.6 million votes. Poll B overprojected Biden by 16,437,711 votes and Trump by 15,974,586 votes. In total, this is an overprojection of approximately 32.4 million votes. Poll A was better than poll B by nearly 18 million votes.

These calculations reveal how sensitive vote projections are to the LVM voter turnout estimates. It is impossible to provide a complete assessment of the performance of a poll without knowing its prediction for voter turnout, and this is not something pollsters disclose. They should.

CHAPTER 11

EACH ELECTION BRINGS SPECIFIC CHALLENGES TO POLLSTERS

PREDICTIVE MODELS DO NOT HAVE TO MAKE SENSE

An economics professor once explained predictive modeling to me. He said the sole criterion for judging these models is their predictive value—not whether they made sense.

The example he used was in grading college test essays. Remember those blue books for essays during exams? Well, one way to grade them, which most colleges at the time used, was to establish rubrics and have teaching assistants grade them all. This process took time and effort.

"What if," my professor pondered, "I could go to the top of the big staircase at the library and toss the blue books down? I could give those that traveled the furthest an A and work my way back up to F for those that did not travel very far. Would that be a defensible way to grade these exams?"

My answer was "Of course not" because I could see no causal reason why those landing at the bottom would be better essays than those at the top. Unless they had longer responses which weighted them down with ink somehow.[135]

My professor pressed on. "But what if when I tossed the blue books down the stairs, they lined up perfectly, from the best essays to the worst? And it worked every time. Would that be an effective grading model?"

He explained that the answer depends on whether you are looking for a predictive or causal model.

With a predictive model, we do not need a coherent reason why tossing the blue books down the stairs gives us a good grading model. It only needs to be shown that the result correlates with the essay's quality.

Yet, we are left with a sour taste in our mouths, wondering why the predictive model works. We need a reason to understand what is happening.

We have covered potential errors that affect all survey research projects and problems specific to pre-election polling. There are other problems to consider: issues particular to the 2016 and 2020 polls. During this time, the media and public lost confidence in pollsters. The 2012 polls were less predictive than those in 2016 and 2020, yet the public did not vilify pollsters in 2012.

Was there something specific to these two elections that caused everyone to turn on the pollsters? What has happened that is unique to 2016 and 2020?

---

135 This is itself a poor model since heavy objects fall at the same speed as light objects.

Not considering the current atmosphere is at the crux of polling's recurring cycle of failure. Pollsters remedied the problems they faced in the 2016 polls in time for 2020. That did not work out well for them, and they are doing the same thing in time for 2024, thinking that will miraculously solve polling's woes. As Einstein remarked, "The definition of insanity is doing the same thing over and over again but expecting different results."

We should look at both internal and external causes to investigate what happened in 2016 and 2020. Internal causes refer to changes *relating to research and polling* since 2012 that could cause a polling misfire. External causes refer to changes that *have happened in the world* that can influence polls. External causes are beyond the pollsters' control, but this does not absolve the pollsters—it is their job to adjust to a changing world.

Let us start with internal causes.

Market research completed its transformation from telephone to online data collection just before the 2012 election cycle. Pollsters have been slower to adopt online data collection than the broader field of market research. Still, many more polls are being done online, and the 2012 election was the first time the bulk of pollsters embraced online polling.

The quality of telephone research centers has declined because of this transformation to online data collection. In my first job, my company maintained a polling call center in the back of our building. Our proximity to the interviewers gave us tight control over how we collected data. We had friendships with interviewers, and research managers would often get on the telephone themselves to conduct polls.

That no longer happens in telephone data collection. Few researchers and pollsters maintain telephone centers because so little telephone research is being done. I do not know of a single pollster with their own telephone center anymore.

Instead, this work is contracted to large phone banks that do not specialize in polling, often operating abroad. Pollsters buy data collection on a cost basis because it is the most significant cost component in a poll. Interviewers are pressed to speed their way through interviews. Quality has suffered.

Another internal cause of problems in 2016 and 2020 is pollsters looking to the past to develop their likely voter models (LVMs). Post-election, the methodologists would discover how they could have weighted the data differently to make a better forecast, and they would apply this knowledge to the next election.

All the weeping and gnashing of teeth that occurred after 2016 caused pollsters to change what they were doing. They changed their sampling to maintain education quotas. They stepped up the quantity of swing-state polls. They tweaked their LVMs.

What happened? A worse polling miss in 2020.

Pollsters learned from 2016 and tweaked their processes for 2020. The result was an optimal way to poll—*in 2016*. The world had moved on. Pollsters failed to see that 2020 was a unique year. They assumed optimizing processes to fix past polling problems would succeed in 2020. The polling generals always seem to want to fight the last war.

Next up are external causes. In addition to issues that apply to polls and their methodology, we need to look at macro issues as possible causes. These macro issues could be the underlying determinants of polling's woes.

Macro issues are always at play in pre-election polling. Election cycles take place within unique historical contexts. The country may be in an overseas conflict or at war. The economy may be booming or crashing. Social unrest could be peaking. Technology could be changing the nature of society. Each election has some aspect of the macro world unique to that time.

Many investment gurus come up with stock-picking models that fit well to past data. Few, if any, have models that effectively predict future stock prices.

Pollsters face the same type of problem—their LVMs model to past data, which may or may not be relevant in a changing world. This would work if the world stood still between elections, which is rarely the case. Polling methods evolve slower than the world they aim to measure.

The 2020 macro environment was complicated. The electorate became more polarized, or at least our politicians did. People took to the streets to call attention to social justice issues. Today's media isolates people from honest debates on issues. The US hegemony in the world is softening or has disappeared. The incumbent president was a divisive figure. The year 2020 was not 2016, and 2024 will not be 2020.

THE PANDEMIC'S INFLUENCE ON 2020 POLLS

One macro factor stands out in 2020: the COVID-19 pandemic. This issue changed how Americans lived their daily lives in 2020. The pandemic disrupted work life, home life, education, healthcare, and the economy.

The 2020 election cycle was dominated by debates over how the government should respond to the pandemic. This was a public health emergency the likes of which the world had not faced in over 100 years.

Backward-fitting LVMs did not have any information to use for their models. I listened to a podcast where a leading data modeler suggested that their 2020 prediction was not optimal because there was no precedent in the data for the COVID-19 public health emergency. He indicated that his model would have been better if polling data had reached as far back as the 1918 Spanish flu pandemic.

This should show just how backward-looking methodologists are when creating their models. Do we think that data from more than a century ago would help our predictions? What we knew about 2016 did not improve our forecasts for 2020, so I am not sure that data from 1918 would have helped.

The COVID-19 pandemic also changed how people physically voted. In the 2020 election, 69% of voters nationwide cast their ballot before Election Day, either by mail or in person.[136] That is

---

136 Zachary Scherer, "Majority of Voters Used Nontraditional Methods to Cast Ballots in 2020," United States Census Bureau, April 29, 2021, https://www.census.gov/library/stories/2021/04/what-methods-did-people-use-to-vote-in-2020-election.html.

a fundamental change. Making voting more accessible and flexible helped increase turnout to two-thirds of voters in 2020.[137]

The ability to vote using different methods across an extended period tested pollsters. If a respondent indicated they would vote early, by mail or in person, pollsters did not have past data to calibrate their models.

A key challenge to pollsters is determining if a person will turn out to vote. What do pollsters do if the person we are surveying has already voted when the poll is fielded? The short answer is, pollsters gave early voters a 100% probability of voting in their models.

But the probability is not 100%. Some early ballots are not postmarked on time. Others may not be filled out correctly and are tossed. Early mail-in voters may turn out on Election Day and cancel their earlier vote. The systems used vary by state. Although we can trust mail-in voting systems, that trust is not 100%.

Mail-in ballots in 2020 favored Democratic candidates. Because mail-in voting favored Biden and a proportion of mail-in votes would prove invalid, this would cause pollsters to overpredict Biden's performance. Not by much, and the polls were not drastically off—the central problem is most were off in the same direction.

Josh Clinton of the 2020 AAPOR task force and professor of

137 Jacob Fabina, "Despite Pandemic Challenges, 2020 Election Had Largest Increase in Voting between Presidential Elections on Record," American Chronicle, April 29, 2021, https://americanchronicle.com/?p=318.

political science at Vanderbilt University concluded that differences in how people voted relating to the pandemic were accounted for by pollsters and are likely not a key reason for inaccuracies in 2020 polling.

> We found that pollsters generally were able to accurately account for how people were going to vote—that is, they didn't end up with too few Election Day voters or too many early voters.[138]

The 2020 COVID-19 pandemic does not explain what happened to the 2016 polls, which took place several years before the pandemic. Or the 2012 polls, which were the poorest performing recent polls (and were biased in favor of Democrats, not Republicans).

There have been fundamental societal changes that have affected the polls since 2008. We should not discount the possibility that the period of 1952–2008 was unique, and there has been a return to a more "normal" historical period.

The last half of the 20th century was remarkably stable. America's world power grew. The political tenor in Washington was one of compromise between political parties. Presidential candidates of that era look moderate compared to those of the past few cycles.

Other eras in US history have had hyperpartisanship. The philosophical differences between the dominant parties were intense during the nation's founding. And it is hard to think of a more

---

138 Scott Keeter, "Q&A: A Conversation about US Election Polling Problems in 2020," Pew Research Center, July 21, 2021, https://www.pewresearch.org/fact-tank/2021/07/21/a-conversation-about-u-s-election-polling-problems-in-2020/.

divisive era in US history than the Antebellum period through Reconstruction, when the country went to war with itself and the threat of a second Civil War was very real.

There were no polls back in the 1800s, but if there were, they would have struggled to predict elections in such a polarized environment. The unpredictability of the current era may not be unique. Pollsters may have been lucky that it was so easy to poll within the Cold War period.

The COVID-19 pandemic affected everybody, but it did not affect everybody equally. COVID-19 infections and deaths have skewed toward men, minorities, older people, and lower-income individuals. The economic impact has not been uniform. Unemployment hit hard in low-income communities and among people working in retail, restaurants, and entertainment.

For the polls, the implication is that COVID-19 did not affect every voter in the same way. Presuming that subgroups of people would behave as they did in 2016 proved a poor assumption. Pollsters in 2020 fixed the problems of 2016 but could not foresee new issues that arose in 2020. There is no reason to believe the tweaks they are contemplating for 2024 will yield better results.

WERE POLLSTERS OUT TO GET TRUMP?

Conservative pundits and pollsters have put forth a story that pollsters missed their election calls in 2016 and 2020 because they conspired against the Trump candidacy. Although I firmly believe this is not the case, the American public believes this narrative.

In the Crux Poll, we asked about polling bias. Forty-one percent of our respondents who had answered a 2020 pre-election poll felt that the survey was biased. Of those, almost two-thirds (65%) felt the poll was biased toward Joe Biden and against Donald Trump.

Eighty-one percent of Trump voters and half (51%) of Biden voters felt that the pre-election poll they took was biased against Trump. The perception that the polls were biased against Trump existed among supporters of both candidates.[139]

Pollsters take umbrage at this insinuation. I have known researchers and pollsters with personal views that span the political spectrum. Although one's background and beliefs subtly influence how they construct surveys, reputable pollsters do not consciously bias their polls. I do not know the political leanings of pollsters I have known for more than 20 years, which is a testament to their integrity. Patrick Murray of Monmouth University wrote:

> I take my responsibility as a public pollster seriously. Some partisan critics think we have some agenda about who wins or loses. I can only assume they have never met a public pollster. The thing that keeps us up at night—our "religion" as it were—is simply getting the numbers right.[140]

---

139   We took great care in the Crux Poll to keep question wording neutral and unbiased. Just 20% of our respondents felt our poll was biased, and about the same number of people felt it was biased in a liberal direction.

140   Patrick Murray, "Pollster: 'I Blew It.' Maybe It's Time to Get Rid of Election Polls," NJ.com, November 4, 2021, https://www.nj.com/opinion/2021/11/pollster-i-blew-it-maybe-its-time-to-get-rid-of-election-polls-opinion.html.

If I have written this book well, you should have no clue about my political leanings. As a pollster, I have to refrain from letting them creep into my interpretations of data. I am sure it happens, but good researchers and pollsters make a considerable effort to prevent it.

Pollsters and researchers are a different breed. External success measures do not inspire them as much as they motivate others. The best researchers I know see business success as a means to an end. Yes, the company needs to make money. But what we care about is that we get it right for our clients.

Researchers are intrinsically motivated people, which is why I hold them in such high regard. The better ones would be working in academia if they were not in market research. Research integrity is central to who they are.

Pollsters have a clear vested interest in getting it right. I have conducted many high-stakes research studies. Millions of dollars and people's careers can be on the line. There tends to be no way of knowing whether these studies make accurate predictions. Good managers view them in a broader context of other information and their specific business situations.

Pre-election polls are different. You do a poll and predict a result. In a few days, the entire world sees how you did.

I have never met a reputable pollster who would publish an inaccurate poll; they have too much on the line. There is no incentive to get it wrong. The notion that a conspiracy exists among pollsters to put out inaccurate polls is absurd. As an insider, I can assure you that this is not the case.

CHAPTER 12

TEN IDEAS FOR FUTURE POLLING SUCCESS

Opinion polls are essential to the functioning of a democratic society. Although they have unduly influenced public opinion at times, George Gallup was correct when he felt that well-constructed opinion polls serve as the best way to keep elected officials accountable to the electorate.

Ironically, polls are struggling at a time when the world has become data-centric. The polls need fixing. Citizens deserve this.

All is not lost for the polls. Humphrey Taylor, the former chairman of the Harris Poll, remarked:

> Well designed, well conducted surveys work. Their record overall is pretty good. Most social, and marketing, researchers would be very happy with the average forecasting errors of the polls...

However, there are enough disasters in the history of election predictions for readers to be cautious about interpreting the results.[141]

Polls are not going anywhere, but they have to get better and be perceived as better. Pollsters must establish trust, and the best way of doing this is by getting better at predicting elections. By predicting elections accurately, pollsters develop confidence in their opinion polls and build their corporate market research businesses. A sizable industry (market research) ultimately depends on the success of pre-election polls.

This section presents 10 ideas that could help improve the polls and our trust in them. Although perhaps none of these ideas can magically cure polling's problems, each could help the polls improve. These are the issues pollsters should be considering, rather than subtle tweaks to their sampling and likely voter models (LVMs).

These suggestions largely share two themes: trust and simplicity. Simply put, the polls are going nowhere if pollsters cannot reestablish trust with those who take them. Pollsters are in a negative cycle where election miscalls seed distrust. This distrust causes response rates to fall, which in turn causes more election miscalls. Pollsters must break this loop.

The cycle will not be disrupted by creating more complex solutions. Instead, pollsters need to get back to the basics and concentrate on simplifying their methods.

---

141 Taylor, "Myth and Reality in Reporting Sampling Error."

IDEA 1: USE BIG-DATA APPROACHES

Immediately after the 2020 election, I had heated email discussions with research colleagues where we tried to decipher what 2020 would mean for market research going forward. My colleagues felt survey research was broken beyond repair, but not to worry because researchers would soon learn how to tap into vast streams of behavioral data to predict elections. Big-data techniques would supplant the need for pre-election polls.

Big data's successes in other contexts set up an expectation that something as simple as an election should be predictable. Amazon recommends products relevant to my needs. Netflix knows what I like to watch better than I do. Facebook has become so efficient at predicting preferences that many people are convinced the company must be spying on them via cameras and microphones on their devices.[142] Google Maps knows better than I do where I have been recently and even where I want to go.

Why not tap into this same brilliance to predict how people will vote?

Many people misunderstand what big data is and what it can do. We live in a data-rich world and, importantly, a world that now has the computing power to store and process enormous datasets. Online behavior is being recorded. The bits and pieces of data left behind by consumers are helpful to marketers.

It is conceivable that big data can better predict how a person will vote than they themself can report on a poll. There very well

<hr>

142 Michael Nunez, "All of the Creepy Things Facebook Knows about You," Gizmodo, August 19, 2016, https://gizmodo.com/all-of-the-creepy-things-facebook-knows-about-you-1785510980.

could be a day where an artificial intelligence predicts voting behavior with greater certainty than a person can. The cyberworld may know you better than you know yourself.

This approach is in use by marketers. They use social media companies' data to predict if you will click on an ad and buy a product. They are finding this can be more predictive than surveys that ask about consumer preferences.

Neuromarketing is a burgeoning field that uses brain science to predict how consumers will react to advertisements and packaging. Neuromarketing is seen by many as manipulative and unethical.[143] It has not taken off because of the expense of using fMRI machines, but it will become widely used once that cost comes down. Insights from neuromarketing will help researchers predict consumer behavior.

Researchers are figuring out how to link various large datasets together. Academics combine IRS income tax records with information from the US Census to understand the social impacts of policy decisions. Public health researchers combine US Census information with online search data to discover disease outbreaks before they are reported to the health system. Google researchers look at search histories to discover global trends that affect poverty and disease. The potential for big data to be a positive force in the world is astonishing.

Although big data threatens traditional pre-election polling, the broader fields of opinion and survey research will survive

---

143   Jason Flores, Arne Baruca, and Robert Saldivar, "Is Neuromarketing Ethical? Consumers Say Yes. Consumers Say No," *Journal of Legal, Ethical and Regulatory Issues* 17, no. 2 (2014): 77–91, https://digitalcommons.sacredheart.edu/wcob_fac/379/.

because they can do things big data cannot. Large behavioral datasets can generate predictive but not causal models. Survey research and polls can delve deep into the underlying motivations of decisions, which is of keen interest to marketers. Marketers, and political observers, want to know *why* people do what they do, not just *what* they will do.

In polling, big data may predict the elections, but polls will always be necessary to understand why the race is shaping up as it is and which issues are of concern to people.

Researchers can look at behavioral patterns to predict what you are likely to do in a given situation. For instance, a researcher can test multiple versions of an online advertisement. The researcher can see which one performed better and analyze the demographic profile and online behavior of those who clicked on the ad. After the test, it is possible to serve the ad to a large targeted audience and predict how many people will click on it.[144] Political fundraisers widely use this approach.[145]

That is a predictive analysis. Data are used to predict future behavior. It is exciting. It is also creepy. It is easy to see how the approach could be adapted to predict voting behavior and election results.

Predicting an election is different than a causal analysis. A causal analysis focuses on understanding why people make the decisions they do. Why did you click on the ad? What about

---

144 This is known as A/B testing.

145 Philippe Aime, "The Secret behind Obama's 2012 Election Success: A/B Testing (No, Really!)," Convertize, November 21, 2016, https://medium.com/convertize/the-secret-behind-obamas-2012-election-success-a-b-testing-no-really-df672c248926.

it was appealing? What needs do you have that a product can fulfill?

These why questions drive marketing strategy and creative direction. Survey research will survive because it answers questions big data cannot and because those answers are central to effective marketing. Marketing managers can ignore these questions in the short term and focus on garnering more clicks, but long-term strategies will drift and fail if they do not delve into underlying causes.

Back to pre-election polling. If researchers do not care *why* people choose a candidate and only want to know *how* they will vote, why not use big data?

In theory, they can. Pollsters have to discover which big-data sources provide voting behavior correlates. Here, we are not worrying about causation. Although it is nice to have an underlying reason to predict election behavior from a metric, it is not the focus.

In statistics, there is a saying that "all models are wrong, but some are useful." Models simplify reality. In that process, they have errors. There is no such thing as a correct model as all have a degree of uncertainty. If they did not have this imprecision, they would not be models; they would be reality.

Using this logic, we do not have to think about causal factors or models making intuitive sense when predicting election results. If I can predict your voting choices by knowing your shoe size, that is great, as long as it works.

In practice, researchers do not like to develop predictive models with no theory behind them. Nobody likes a model that does not make sense. There is underlying reasoning behind them.

David Wasserman from the Cook Political Report developed an interesting one.[146] Wasserman discovered that voting districts with a Whole Foods were more likely to vote Democratic, and those with a Cracker Barrel were more likely to vote Republican. Underlying this prediction was that Whole Foods and Cracker Barrels locate in distinct demographic areas and can serve as proxies for the demographics of the surrounding voting population.

I attended an AAPOR conference after the 2000 election (Bush versus Gore), where a researcher from the US Census Bureau presented a similar analysis. Instead of Whole Foods and Cracker Barrel, he used Starbucks and Walmart. Knowing whether Starbucks or Walmart was closer to the election site was predictive of which candidate that site would favor.

Perhaps predicting election success may be as simple as choosing the right retailers.

Do not slough this type of prediction off too quickly. As near as I can tell, a model that uses the Whole Foods/Cracker Barrel divide is at least as effective at predicting presidential election outcomes as polling.

---

146 David Wasserman, "To Beat Trump, Democrats May Need to Break Out of the 'Whole Foods' Bubble," *The New York Times*, March 3, 2020, https://www.nytimes.com/interactive/2020/02/27/upshot/democrats-may-need-to-break-out-of-the-whole-foods-bubble.html.

On the Crux Poll, we used three pairs of retailers and found high correlations between them and voting behavior:

- If you indicate you live closer to a Trader Joe's than a Dollar Store, there is a 53% chance you voted for Biden, a 30% chance you voted for Trump, a 6% chance you voted for someone else, and an 11% chance you did not vote.
- If you indicate you live closer to a Starbucks than a Walmart, there is a 51% chance you voted for Biden, a 29% chance you voted for Trump, a 5% chance you voted for someone else, and a 15% chance you did not vote.
- If you indicate you live closer to a Whole Foods than a Cracker Barrel, there is a 47% chance you voted for Biden, a 28% chance you voted for Trump, a 4% chance you voted for someone else, and a 21% chance you did not vote.

A researcher can combine these results with a dataset that shows which voting districts fall into each retail camp to create estimates of who will win the election.

Demographics matter because they are predictive of voting behavior. Big-data approaches have access to detailed demographic data.

A limitation of the approach is that the biggest data available come from privately owned online behavioral datasets (companies like Google and Facebook). A system using those datasets would work well if every likely voter had online access and spewed a similar amount of data contrails as they lived their lives, but they do not. Statistical gurus will take some time to make these models viable. Big data will likely change how pre-election polling is conducted.

There will always be a need for survey research in pre-election polling because understanding why people choose a candidate provides the basis for candidate platforms, pundit pontification, and water cooler discussions everywhere.

Pioneers of early polling saw little value in predicting elections. Election predictions were a nuisance but a helpful litmus test to prove that the methodologies used for opinion polling worked. What mattered to the early pollsters was compelling candidates to assess the viability of their positions and adjust them to the will of the populace. They viewed polls as a public service.

A person's current intent and attitudes (measured by survey research) may prove more predictive of voting behavior than their past behavior (measured by big data). Selzer & Company's success underscores that intentions can be more relevant than past behavior. Big data models the past.

Errors in pre-election polls have more to do with response rates and predicting voter turnout than with the questions posed. In the short term, expect to see big data used to improve voter turnout predictions. Let me give an example.

Demographic questions are essential to LVMs. Pollsters need to ask about age, sex/gender, religion, political party affiliation, education, income, and so forth to weight the data and predict whether a person will turn out to vote. These questions are critical inputs to LVMs. Most analyses of pre-election polling failures concentrate on the demographic composition of the samples.

These questions are uncomfortable. The race and income

questions are the most refused questions on any survey. Demographic questions are presented late in a survey when the person answering the poll is tired. A typical poll is about 20 minutes long and tedious.

Demographic questions are not as reliable[147] as researchers think. The first research seminar I attended (in 1990) was on measurement errors in survey research. I remember a presenter showing how the income question's design affected results. The categories affected the response.[148]

In statistical jargon, this means the income question has poor reliability. Researchers get different answers depending on how it is posed. This inconsistency is problematic for pollsters since income is crucial input for an LVM. Pollsters are using an unstable input.

Considerable discussion about setting quotas for education categories took place after the 2016 election. Most pollsters did so in 2020. The education question was included twice in the Crux Poll to test reliability—once early in the survey and once toward the end. People answered the question twice about 10 minutes apart.

A measure such as education should have reliability. We should get the same answer no matter where it is asked on a questionnaire or if someone is interviewed at different times.

---

147 In a statistical sense, a "reliable" measure is one where you get a consistent response every time you ask it.

148 This researcher showed that when presented with income categories, people tend to assume that the categories in the middle were average or normal and where typical people should answer. Regardless of the actual incomes presented, middle-income respondents had a tendency to pick something in the middle of the range.

For the education question, on the Crux Poll, we found that 92% of poll takers gave the same response early and late in the questionnaire, and 8% did not.

The education question pollsters hoped would remedy 2016 issues in time for 2020 is not a perfectly reliable measure. In the Crux Poll, one in 12 people provided unreliable data for this question.

Once more, the 8% who provided unreliable data were skewed toward the lower education categories. This is the subgroup that 2020 pollsters were weighting upward—those who provided the least reliable information on their educational backgrounds. Weighting them upward magnified the error.

Another question that seems simple but is not is asking for a person's sex. Most studies ask people if they are male or female. This question is no longer as straightforward as it once was, as social norms are evolving, and many people no longer view sex as binary.[149] Beyond sex, concepts of gender and sexual identity are important to consider, not just for inclusion but because these concepts correlate strongly with voting behavior.

Pollsters seek to predict voter behavior. Voter behavior correlates with a broader range of sex, gender, and identification categories, so pollsters should gather these variables in a more detailed and inclusive manner. Few pollsters do so.

Demographic questions are the most consequential inputs into

149 See "The Evolution of Demographic Questions: New Position Paper from the Insights Association IDEA Council," The Insights Association, 2021, https://logicaresearch.com/the-evolution-of-demographic-questions/.

LVMs, yet gathering them on polls is not as straightforward as it seems. Big data can help.

A big-data approach can track answers on other surveys and online behavior to predict how individuals should answer these questions. These predictions can be more accurate than poll responses. Big data can help determine if people answer these crucial questions accurately.

Big data can look for inconsistencies. Suppose you respond that you will vote for Joe Biden over Donald Trump. Yet, your data profile shows you have surfed message boards promoting Second Amendment rights, you spend hours weekly watching Fox News political commentators, and you have posted pictures of yourself at Trump rallies. That would raise red flags in the data that you perhaps have not answered honestly.

The depth of your involvement in these activities can clue a researcher into your propensity to show up and vote on Election Day. Predicting turnout is where pre-election polls falter—pollsters all have unique ways of predicting who will show up. No standard exists on how to do so.

It is easy to envision a time when researchers know so much about where you have been, what you watch, and what you engage in online that a poll will not be needed to know whom you will vote for and whether you will vote. We are moving in this direction, but there are so many issues relating to developing these models and privacy that it will be a long time before it happens.

IDEA 2: PREDICTION MARKETS—PUTTING YOUR MONEY WHERE YOUR OPINION IS

A movement is afoot to allow Nevada casinos to take bets on presidential elections.[150] Wagering on who will be the next president might increase interest in the election and voter turnout. It will also draw more revenue to the casinos.

Detractors of this idea cite the typical arguments against gambling of any kind. I suppose campaign insiders could engineer a campaign emergency to sabotage their candidate and collect winning bets they have made on the other side.

But will betting on elections result in better predictions than current polling methods?

Pre-election polling is basic. Pollsters find a representative sample of likely voters. They ask a straightforward question: if the election were held today, for whom would you vote? While the question itself is simple, polls often disagree on the answers. Differences in the polls stem from how the sample was drawn, how "likely voters" are classified, and context (questions that may have preceded the voting question).

Pollsters are not always right. If polling organizations were to select presidents, our children would be learning about the policies of Presidents Alf Landon, Thomas Dewey, Al Gore, and Hillary Clinton.

A few election cycles back, some firms tried a new approach. Rather than ask "Whom would you vote for?" the new approach

---

150 Katy Steinmetz, "Bet on Red! Nevada May Legalize Gambling on Federal Elections," *Time*, March 27, 2013, https://www.tick4nevada.com/bet-on-red-nevada-may-legalize-gambling-on-federal-elections/.

asked, "Regardless of whom you may favor or vote for, who do you think will win the election?" This was an attempt to get over the difficulty of predicting turnout. It was a way to crowdsource a pre-election poll.

The approach worked but has been tried too infrequently to make a definitive judgment on its efficacy. Pre-election polls are great experiments. Their success can be judged against a real-world result.

A new approach to the last few election cycles was taken by online betting sites, such as Betfair, PredictIt, and the now-defunct Intrade. These are "prediction markets"—exchanges that trade shares for future events with a "yes/no"-type outcome.

For instance, there can be a trade event for "Will Barack Obama win the election?" The share price for this would be between $0 and $1. Once the election is over, a share of Obama would close at $1 if he won and $0 if he lost.

Since an active market in this trading existed, a person could make real bets with real money on the election. For instance, if an Obama share was trading at 72 cents, this implies the market feels he has a 72% chance of winning. If you thought Obama had a greater than 72% chance of winning, you would buy his "stock," which would pressure the price upward. When the election was over, you would either lose 72 cents per share if he lost the election or make 28 cents per share if he won.

Watching how candidate stock prices moved as the campaign season progressed was captivating. A candidate's share price would change after the conventions or debates. At any moment, the share price implied the probability of victory. A rousing speech would move a candidate's price (and the likelihood of winning) up a few points. The impact of real-world events showed up faster in the prediction markets than in the polls.

Allowing Vegas-style betting on presidential elections would be fascinating. But would it be accurate?

According to law professor Richard Posner, prediction markets can be better than polls:

> An interesting comparison between the Gallup Poll and the Iowa market in the 1996 presidential campaign reveals that throughout the entire campaign the Iowa market predicted outcome was much closer (in margin of victory) to the actual outcome than the Gallup Poll was. Studies have found that prediction markets beat polls and other prediction tools even when a prediction market uses play rather than real money.[151]

Prediction markets act as an efficient tax on misinformation or "fake news." If a bettor believes an irrelevant or untrue fact, they become the "dumb money" at the table, benefiting those who properly value information sources. Those working off honest, vetted information sources are at an advantage.

Vegas bookmakers establish initial odds on an event. These odds (or a point spread, in the case of football) evolve depending on how the betting comes in. Oddsmakers are not concerned about the probability of who might win a sporting event. Instead, they

---

151   Richard Posner, "Prediction Markets and the Election—Posner," *The Becker-Posner Blog*, September 14, 2008, https://www.becker-posner-blog.com/2008/09/prediction-markets-and-the-election--posner.html.

set and adjust odds/point spreads to attract an even amount of money bet on both teams, as that is how the casino maximizes profits. The spread might not reflect the probability of winning, especially for teams with large, rabid fan bases, who may irrationally wager on their team (providing a buying opportunity for the rest of us).

How do the Vegas oddsmakers do? In a perfect world (from the casino's point of view), 50% of underdogs would win, and 50% of favorites would win. In 2013, teams played 512 regular-season NFL games. Favorites won 248 times (48.9%). This figure is not statistically different than 50%, so it appears the sportsbooks do an excellent job.

Allowing Vegas casinos to take election bets could result in a better prediction than the pre-election polls. Money flows in response to new information and may behave more rationally than individual respondents in a poll. The polling organizations will not go out of business because polls have a unique capability to understand who voted for whom and why, and survey results drive campaign decisions and news content.

In May 2007, 25 leading thinkers in economics, the AEI Brookings Joint Center for Regulatory Studies, released a statement arguing:

> US regulators should lower barriers to the creation and design of prediction markets by creating a safe harbor for certain types of small stakes markets. We believe our proposed change has the potential to stimulate innovation in the design and use of prediction markets throughout the economy, and in the process

to provide information that will benefit the private sector and government alike.[152]

There are Nobel Laureates in this group of thinkers. Prediction markets have some brilliant minds on their side.

Prediction markets are subject to the same irrationality that can occur in financial markets. They require extensive regulation. The markets would have to have a robust activity level to become efficient.

When there is not much activity level, the prediction markets do not work well. In early December 2020, the prediction market PredictIt still had Donald Trump with a 12% chance of winning the election. Later, after a Supreme Court decision killed any chance of him contesting the election, this market still was trading at a 5% likelihood of Trump winning.

Within a week of the election in 2020, the actual probability of a Biden victory became known, and his odds should have approached 100% in these markets, but it did not. Some bettors were still putting money on Trump.

This behavior may be a commentary on the lack of objectivity of news sources and the electorate's gullibility. The concern is whether these prediction markets can forecast election winners. One potential downside to prediction markets is that it might be too difficult to vet the credibility of the information sources

---

152   Kenneth J. Arrow et al., "Statement on Prediction Markets," *Macroeconomics eJournal* (2007), https://www.semanticscholar.org/paper/Statement-on-Prediction-Markets-Arrow-Sunder/89b5b3ce906fcc3e578c6f074329b80da18190f5.

that are central to their efficient operation. Markets rely on trusted information.

Although some of us would look at this as an opportunity to make money (like taking advantage of neophytes at a poker table), it should draw into question the ability of prediction markets to forecast winning probabilities. A prediction market needs many rational actors and free-flowing accurate information to make efficient predictions. As interest in them grows, prediction markets may become a viable way to predict elections.

IDEA 3: STOP DOING POLLS TOO EARLY

College football is a sizable business. According to *Forbes*, "the sport's 25 most valuable programs combine to earn an average of $1.5 billion in profit on annual revenues of $2.7 billion."[153] That is an insane profit percentage (56%), but that is what happens when a business does not pay its workers (the players).

Crowning a national champion in college football is not as meritorious as it is in other sports. In college basketball, 68 teams compete in a tournament to determine the national champion. In track and field, the fastest athletes all line up in one track meet to see who is the best. Each year the nation's top 64 college baseball teams travel to Omaha to play in a tournament to decide which team is the national champion.

College football is different. Football players take such a phys-

---

153 Chris Smith, "College Football's Most Valuable Teams: Reigning Champion Clemson Tigers Claw into Top 25," *Forbes*, September 12, 2019, https://www.forbes.com/sites/chrissmith/2019/09/12/college-football-most-valuable-clemson-texas-am/?sh=2d74ecc5a2e7.

ical pounding each week that they cannot play more than a dozen or so games each year. Even if the NCAA could run a 68-team college football tournament, recovery times for the players after each game would result in the tournament taking the entire semester to complete.

There is pressure to declare a national college football champion each year. Until 1993, a poll of college football experts chose these champions. The first college football poll was established in 1901.[154] There were two polls throughout the '80s and '90s, the AP and the UPI. The two did not always agree on who was champion.[155] College football fans (and sports talk hosts) had difficulty stomaching that their championship was subjectively determined.

The current ranking system for college football was established in 2004 after several false starts. This system empowers a committee to rank the teams. This committee considers a mix of polls of college football experts and a complex formula of game statistics to rank teams.

The top four teams face off in a two-game tournament at the end of the season. Although seen as an improvement, this still sparks debate on whether the system gets the correct teams into this tournament.

The college football system is imperfect, but starting in 2014, they began to do something right that pollsters can learn from: they stopped publicizing rankings early in the season.

---

154 The College Football Historian, 2008. Internet resource.

155 The two polls differed on the national champion in both 1990 and 1991.

Early season rankings unfairly benefit programs with solid legacies and that play well the prior year. This does not make sense, given that at least 25% of a team's players graduate or leave the program each year. These early rankings influenced later rankings. A team ranked #20 early had virtually no chance at ending up at #1 even if the team had a historically good season.

It has varied, but college football rankings are published in weeks nine or ten of a 16-week college football season. Waiting until midway through the season gives teams a chance of a fair ranking.[156]

There is a clear analogy for pollsters. Early polling is not only not very predictive of outcomes, but it is unfair to lesser-known candidates. The days of unknown candidates ascending to the presidency (Jimmy Carter, Bill Clinton) are likely over because so many polls are conducted too early.

Because of early polling, an outsider to politics would have difficulty becoming a viable presidential candidate unless they have built a reputation in advance. This difficulty is unfortunate, as polls should mirror the nation's views. Instead, early polls are a magnet drawing attention to known candidate brands.

Early polls create problems. They make it challenging for lesser-known candidates to raise money. They contribute to an elongation of the campaign season, which is currently around two full years. Early polls lead public opinion rather than reflect it.

---

156 But not all. In 2017, the University of Central Florida went 12–0 on their season and still was not selected to participate in the College Football Playoff.

Pollsters predict elections insanely early. I first noticed polls for the 2024 primaries in October 2020—before the 2020 election had even been held. That would be like conducting a college football poll for the following year sometime between the end of the previous year's regular season and the championship game.

Leading media brands need to form a consortium. This consortium would include the media brands with enormous audiences, like broadcast TV networks, cable news networks, key radio brands, top podcasts, leading newspapers, and online news sources and influencers with large followings. These are the news brands concerned about their reputation. They have fact-checking operations in place.

This "media club" would agree on the earliest possible dates for pre-election poll releases, perhaps a few weeks before primary elections and a few months before general elections. This club would agree to abide by standards for polls or develop their own. Ideally, they would band together to fund polls so pollsters would have the resources needed to do them right.

The college football national championship was decided haphazardly for years because a legacy system was in place. Various major football conferences had too much of a vested interest in the status quo. With a few misstarts, these conferences came together for their mutual benefit when millions of dollars were at stake. Some thought it could not happen, but it did.

The same can happen in the media world.

IDEA 4: ENCOURAGE A POLLING ARCHIVE

Science moves forward in a spirit of openness when it comes to data. Scientists run experiments, publish results, and their peers build on their successes and failures. Science is not about discovering facts as much as it is a method of inquiry that allows us to build on existing knowledge.

Pollsters lack this open scientific spirit. Polling organizations are mostly for-profit companies, and even college polling centers face financial pressures. These pressures work against the scientific openness necessary to improve the polls. It is not profitable to share learnings across organizations.

This is especially true in private market research conducted for companies. An amazing amount of research on consumer behavior and attitudes is being done each year that never sees the light of day. A study is done, the company uses the results to make decisions, and nobody else ever sees the insights. I would estimate that of the 3,000 survey research projects I have been involved in, perhaps 100 of them have been seen beyond a handful of people.

This is a shame because it limits the progress of many fields. The polling field would be much more developed if there were not unnecessary secrecy behind what we learn from our studies.

Earlier, I stated the polling field would be well served if AAPOR became more stringent on its standards for public opinion polls and if media clients would only report on polls that met those standards. One standard should be that a pollster is required to release poll results to a repository, so research into polling can help the field progress.

The Roper Center for Public Opinion Research[157] is an excellent repository of public opinion and election polls housed at Cornell University. It has existed since 1947. Academic researchers use it. Pollsters do not use it nearly as much as they should. When I worked at a major pollster, just a handful of people in our firm knew the Roper Center existed.

I am proposing that pollsters agree to submit polls to the Roper Center as part of their AAPOR membership and that the media refuse to report on polls that fail to take this step.

A "publication bias" exists with pre-election polls. Publication bias refers to when scientists fail to publish articles that do not support their hypotheses. It is a pernicious problem in pharmaceutical research. A drug company might fund an academic researcher to study the efficacy of a new drug. If the study shows the drug does not work, it is less likely to be published than if the study shows the drug *does* work.

Scientists are less likely to make their "failures" public, but much is learned by studies that do not go as planned.

A form of this happens in polling conducted for public relations departments. A company will commission a poll because they want data that frame their product in a good light. Many polling firms design studies to provide a storyline for PR departments to use.

Researchers thread an ethical needle when working on these studies. We make it clear that by attaching our brand to the project, the client must conduct the study in an unbiased, objective

157 The Roper Center for Public Opinion Research, Cornell University, https://ropercenter.cornell.edu/.

manner, and we must approve all press releases resulting from the poll. We guard against clients cherry-picking results—publishing only favorable data points when other parts of the study fail to support their narrative. If anyone contacts us, our clients must allow us to release the entire dataset.

However, a client can bury the entire study and not publish it. Some do. There have been cases where clients have buried the poll, only to recommission a second poll with another firm that only presents the cherry-picked items from the first poll.

The notion of publication bias is a problem in the public opinion world. The AAPOR committee that studied the 2016 polls asked 46 polling organizations to submit their polls for analysis. Roughly half complied. The half that refused to comply conducted polls that contributed to the 2016 polling miss, yet the AAPOR committee could not review their polls to determine why.

This lack of cooperation could be a contributing factor to why the 2016 AAPOR conclusions were more optimistic than expected. Only the most responsible pollsters gave the AAPOR committee the necessary data to do their job.

In its inquiry into the 2019 polls in Australia, the Association of Market and Social Research Organisations and the Statistical Society of Australia lamented that "the lack of access to datasets and detailed descriptions of the survey methods and statistical techniques used by the pollsters materially affected our ability to identify the specific factors that contributed to the inaccuracy of the polls."[158]

---

158 Darren Pennay, et al., "Inquiry into the Performance of the Opinion Polls at the 2019 Australian Federal Election," Association of Market and Social research Organisations, May 2020, https://apo.org.au/sites/default/files/resource-files/2020-05/apo-nid306104.pdf.

To guard against this, AAPOR members should submit all pre-election polls that meet their methodological standards to the Roper Center. Polling organizations should be able to do so without associating their polling brands with the polls if they choose.

Studies that miss their marks need reviewing as much as those that perform well to move polling science forward. Currently, the archive of available pre-election polls suffers from a survivorship bias.

Academics who study polls are bright, but they cannot do their jobs well if they work with half of the data tied behind their backs. Let us give it all to them.

IDEA 5: DEVELOP TRUSTED POLLING BRANDS

Trust in pollsters is low. Since 1988, the Pew Research Center has conducted polls that ask voting-age Americans to grade the way pollsters conducted themselves during the presidential campaigns.[159] There has never been much confidence in pollsters, but 2016 marked a turning point where most people (51%) gave pollsters a failing grade of D or F.

This lack of public confidence in pollsters is accelerating. The Crux Poll indicated that (in 2021) just 17% of US adults trust pollsters/polling organizations. Only 21% of US adults felt that polling organizations did an "excellent" or "good" job in predicting the 2020 US presidential election.

---

159 "Low Marks for Major Players in 2016 Election—Including the Winner," Pew Research Center, November 21, 2016, https://www.pewresearch.org/politics/2016/11/21/low-marks-for-major-players-in-2016-election-including-the-winner/.

Trust in pollsters is directly related to their performance in predicting elections. Modeling the Crux Poll data showed that if all Americans "strongly agreed" that presidential election polls do a good job of predicting who will win, trust in pollsters/polling organizations would increase by 44 million adults. If Americans felt "extremely confident" that pollsters would accurately predict the 2024 election, trust in pollsters would increase by an additional 40 million adults.[160]

Trust in pollsters is possible. We used to have it. Pollsters can start by getting better at what they do: predict election results.

We are in a difficult era for pollsters. The Crux Poll showed that 51% of Americans feel that presidential election polls are getting less accurate over time. Just 12% are confident polling organizations will correctly predict the next president in 2024.

Sure, pollsters can claim they have not done all that poorly in the past two elections and that their results are within a margin of error. They might be statistically correct to do so.

However, "statistical significance" is not why the public does not trust pollsters. They base their trust on whether pollsters pick the winning candidate. This trust is what ultimately matters to the long-term viability of the polls.

Establishing a brand is a key way to build trust. Marketers have spirited debates about what a brand is. Most settle on a definition that encapsulates trust and keeping its promises to customers.

---

160 Thanks to George Terhanian at Electric Insights for creating this model and uncovering this insight.

Brands are effective and valuable because they set expectations. You can be assured a car will be of high quality if it is a Mercedes. A product will be cool if you buy it from Apple. Ben & Jerry's? The ice cream will be decadent and socially responsible at the same time.

Brands have personalities and promises. For many companies, brands are the most valuable asset on their balance sheet. Establishing a well-trusted brand raises the amount a marketer can charge for a product. A strong brand keeps competitors at bay.

Companies obsess over their brand. Considerable spending is geared toward understanding brands and learning how to build them. It is no accident that "brand manager" is a respected marketing job title. Brands are manageable assets.

Brands can make mistakes and become known for negative reasons. This can happen quickly. Kodak was known as a brand that was alongside you during the most emotional times of your life ("Kodak moments"). Now it is known as a case study of how a century-old global brand can lose its footing in a short time.

Consumers value brands for good reasons. Brands save them time and energy searching for new products, assure quality and consistency, and distinguish products from competitors. Consumers like the reliability brands provide. Brands give consumers confidence in the choices they make.

Pollsters lack this trust. Polling brands should stand for methodological rigor, impartial interpretations, and accurate predictions. Although pollsters might think these perceptions already exist, polling brands are largely unknown outside of those working in polling or market research.

The Crux Poll showed that only 11% of Americans could name a pollster. When showed a list of leading pollsters, none garnered more than 50% awareness. Gallup was recognized by just 43% of Americans. Harris was identified by just 16%.

This lack of pollster awareness is a problem and an opportunity. US polling brands are not currently well established, and polling is a fragmented industry with many firms taking part. The situation is ripe for some brands to emerge as leaders.

The success of college polling centers and the Iowa Poll are in no small part due to brand. These brands have become trustworthy. By doing good work, they establish a positive feedback loop that builds their brands further. But these brands have limited reach.

Establishing a brand is expensive. Because polling firms are small organizations, the odds are low one will have the resources to develop a nationally trusted brand quickly. Brand building requires long-term investment.

For this reason, it is unlikely a new trusted polling brand will emerge quickly. Gallup is the one brand that could establish this brand trust, but the Gallup Organization has chosen to sit out pre-election polling for now.

That is a shame, as George Gallup viewed pre-election polling as the ultimate proving ground for opinion polling and market research. The founder of the Gallup Organization never shied away from the challenge of predicting elections, even amid some high-profile mistakes. Those currently running the company that bears his name have quit the pre-election polling business.

Polls need an attachment to other trusted brands because polling organizations do not have the fiscal muscle to do this. We need to think outside the box to find these attachments.

One idea is to have a media organization partner with a pollster. Major media organizations have done this. Trust in media is currently low, so this is not an association pollsters should seek, but lack of media trust has not always been the case.

The media have their own trust issues. They are likely to invest considerably to reestablish trust, and the polling field could hop along for this ride. There is likely a commercial interest in a media brand becoming known as impartial and fair. For this reason, some media brands will emerge strong despite the current atmosphere of mistrust for them.

People want a trusted news source. Having trusted polls can be part of this reemergence. The consumer demand is there.

Even established polling firms have unknown brands. Partnering with stronger media brands for pre-election polling has the effect of watering down a pollster's brand as an independent source because people no longer perceive the media as independent. These polling partnerships are only as strong as the media part of the partnership.

We can think broader.

A polling firm could partner with a well-regarded brand from the corporate world. There would be benefits on both sides of the relationship. The polling firm would gain trust. Users of its polling data would parlay this goodwill to get more market research business. The corporate partner would become seen as genuinely caring about what America thinks, which would help their brand-building efforts.

What brands might work for this? The ideal brand would pervade US life, be trusted, and not be attached to politics. Trust would have to be at its brand core. This brings to mind brands in financial services, medicine, technology, and education.

Currently, the college polling centers are the closest to this. Yet, although fine institutions, the colleges running these centers are regional and not nationally known brands. College polling centers house some excellent pollsters, but their college brands are not broad enough for what I have in mind.

I would like to see the nation's most trusted colleges and universities establish polling centers. Having a university like Princeton, Stanford, or Harvard behind a pre-election poll would give it instant credibility. Leading institutions are unlikely to do this, as the risk of being raked over the embers because of a missed election call is not worth it.

A government agency could provide opinion polling data. It could be difficult for this agency to maintain immunity from political pressures, which would be essential for this to work.

Many of the best, most objective datasets available today are gathered by agencies such as the Census Bureau, the US Bureau of Labor Statistics, the Centers for Disease Control and Prevention, and the Bureau of Justice. Data from government agencies are widely used among researchers and academics and are high quality and impartial.

America once trusted pollsters to tell us how we collectively thought about issues. George Gallup, Elmo Roper, Archibald Crossley, and Louis Harris were not merely pollsters. They were also media personalities who wrote regular, trusted columns syndicated to major newspapers. They made many appearances on radio and television. They did not merely conduct the polls. They became trusted voices to communicate poll results.

America trusted Walter Cronkite, Peter Jennings, Dan Rather, and Tom Brokaw to tell us the news. That time has passed. Who does America trust now to tell us what America thinks?

We could think out of the box as well. Polling organizations could partner with an influencer. This type of alliance sounds ludicrous on the surface, but many of the strongest brands in the world partner with celebrity endorsers.

The "Walter Cronkite Poll," had it existed, would have been very trusted in the 1970s. The "Alex Trebek Poll" would have worked well over the past 20 years. America would have trusted the "man with all the answers" to attach his brand to high-quality opinion polls.

Who now?

We asked in the Crux Poll. We asked about the trustworthiness of 33 individuals, including news personalities, entertainers, athletes, and famous businesspeople. More than half of Americans trusted the following individuals: Morgan Freeman, Dolly Parton, Anthony Fauci, Dwayne "The Rock" Johnson, Michelle Obama, Neil deGrasse Tyson, and Sanjay Gupta.

There are always trusted individuals. This type of partnership can lend credibility to the pollster and provide the influencer with a broader audience.

Unfortunately, public trust in media personalities is low. The Crux Poll asked about 11 media personalities—the anchors and prime time hosts for all major television networks and cable channels. Not a single one of them had a trust level over 50%.

The first polling brands were built on the personae of charismatic founders. Americans had faith in the polls for over 50 years because they were attached to these individuals and their legacies. A charismatic pollster could emerge and resurrect this spirit.

There needs to be a shakeout in polling where a few trusted brands survive. There are too many polls of varying quality. This fragmentation harms all pollsters.

When a market is fragmented, the handful of firms that construct strong brands triumph. Polling is no different. I would guide current pollsters to prepare to invest significantly in their brands or get out of polling altogether.

The public's perception of pollsters might change if there were not so many polls to sort through and a handful of trusted brands existed. That might be a retreat to how it was in the '70s and '80s when elections were not as close and the pollsters got their predictions right.

IDEA 6: DEVELOP TRUSTED POLLING REFEREES

There were more than 1,000 pre-election polls released during the 2020 presidential campaign. Many of these polls were from reputable polling organizations with excellent methods. Some of these polls were untrustworthy. With so many polls released, how do we know which ones to trust?

We need a polling referee.

Polling trade organizations, particularly AAPOR, have a role to play here. Trade organizations establish standards, and reputable pollsters ensure that their polls meet those standards. Current standards have little enforcement mechanism. The polling process is self-policing. It is a case of a fox guarding a henhouse; with the polling organizations banding together to develop the standards, they rarely censure one of their own.

A stamp of approval from a referee might not matter to consumers, but pollsters should work to make adherence to standards more meaningful to the media. Media organizations should want the polls they report to be accurate and conducted to a high standard.

Large media companies have standards and practices departments that review advertising before it airs. Did you know if you want to air an advertisement on national broadcast media that makes a claim based on market research, you have to submit the market research study to them for review? If the survey has a poor methodology, the networks reject the ad.

It is crazy that these same media organizations fail to do something similar for the polls they report. Why not have a review process for polls?[161]

FiveThirtyEight has become a de facto referee for the polls. This nonpartisan organization is part of ABC News and takes an objective approach to polls.

FiveThirtyEight assigns pollsters grades[162] that reflect their past performance. These grades have begotten tighter scrutiny for polls. They have also contributed to herding,[163] as pollsters worry about releasing nonconforming polls for fear of their FiveThirtyEight grade declining.

News organizations should mandate that pollsters disclose their FiveThirtyEight letter grades on all press releases.

This would be like going to a restaurant in New York City. New York has chain restaurants, but many restaurants are single-owner establishments with a tiny brand presence. This lack of awareness makes it hard for travelers to know which restaurants are worth patronizing or even safe. Restaurant brands have low awareness.

The New York County Health Department makes all restaurants display their health grade in their front window. Does anyone

---

161 Some but not all major media organizations have polling editors that serve this function. They ensure that polls released by the media organization meet standards. These editors do not seem to succeed in preventing poor-quality polls from other organizations from being discussed by their journalists and pundits.

162 "FiveThirtyEight's Pollster Ratings."

163 I would like to see FiveThirtyEight provide a measure of herding for pollsters. Pollsters should be releasing polls at least one in 20 times that seem to be outliers. How often are they doing so would tell us if they are failing to release polls.

go into a New York City restaurant graded below an A by the health department? If I see an A in the window, at least I know the food is safe. Ratings provide trust where strong brands do not exist.

There are thousands of polls and dozens of pollsters. I pay close attention to this. I still find excellent polls from organizations I do not recognize and poor-quality polls from organizations I have known for years. Having a trusted, external referee would boost confidence in an unknown polling brand, just as the health inspection rating or Zagat or Yelp feedback reassures diners trying a new restaurant.

An organization like a polling aggregator or a leading university could become the polling referee. This idea is unlikely to resonate with consumers, but it might matter to the media. What media organization that seeks objectivity would ever want to report on a poll with a poor grade from an academic referee?[164]

A referee is needed because the media do not treat polls like other news sources. Major media outlets do not report on unverified sources, yet they frequently report on polls with poor methodology. Although larger media entities have polling editors, it sometimes seems like they are powerless as poor-quality polls slip through and gain airtime.

Even though I like the concept of a polling referee, the sad truth is, referees in all contexts are currently under fire.[165] In sports,

---

164 This begs the question of why FiveThirtyEight uses polls from pollsters they give poor grades to in their election forecasts? These polls are weighted downward but should not be included at all.

165 The author Michael Lewis has an excellent podcast that discusses how referees in many contexts have lost power and respect—https://atrpodcast.com/.

professional athletes, coaches, and commentators constantly complain about calls. I have attended youth soccer and hockey games where parents of 10-year-old children threatened teenage referees.

The lack of trust in referees has not happened solely in sports. Regulators have lost power and respect. Judges are criticized and threatened. People no longer see the media as an unbiased arbiter of truth. There has been a trend toward disrespect for individuals and organizations that enforce rules.

Although establishing a polling referee is a good idea, the country is perhaps not ready. But times change, and I can see the concept of a polling referee taking hold in the future.

IDEA 7: COMPEL THE MEDIA TO STOP REPORTING POOR-QUALITY POLLS

You would be unlikely to see a national news anchor state the story they were about to report was based on an unreliable source they could not confirm, and then report the story. They do the equivalent with polls all the time.

During the 2004 election cycle, Tom Brokaw reported on a call-in poll NBC news conducted. He began with a disclaimer, stating the poll was unscientific, and then reported on the poll anyway.

This same mistake happens over and over among world-class journalists. Why on earth would a journalist report on a poll they know has poor methodology behind it?

Polls are not a specialized "beat" in news organizations. Large news organizations assign reporters to areas when a beat requires technical knowledge. These beats include healthcare, technology, business, sports, and so forth.

Despite being a complex field, polls are not seen as requiring specially trained journalists who understand their subtleties. The news anchor does not forecast the weather, which is because meteorology is a technical skill that requires considerable training. Key individuals in polling organizations are experts in social science research and statistics. Most journalists reporting their work are not.

The result is, some polls of questionable quality receive airtime.

Let us think of a disastrous way to design a pre-election poll. We will start by doing it in a single geographic location—a place spanning a few acres in size. We will conduct this poll more than a year before the election. Let us permit the candidates to attend this event and try to influence the respondents. Candidates can put trade show–like booths up, make speeches, have live entertainment in these booths, and give things away. Finally, let us make the people who take this poll pay $30 to cast their ballot.

This is not the best way to set up a poll. Responsible media would not cover this, would they?

I have described the Iowa Straw Poll, which takes place at the Iowa State Fair in Ames every four years. Virtually every major media outlet in the United States reports on it. This "poll" is held early in the campaign and results in viable candidates dropping out of the race before debates are held or primary votes are cast.

The media extensively covers the Iowa Straw Poll. The lead-up to it is even covered. In the 2020 cycle, I saw pundits on CNN have a serious discussion about its implication to the Democratic candidate field.

Let us design an even more ridiculous poll. Instead of adults, let us have schoolchildren answer the poll. A few weeks before the election, this poll will allow schools to register and participate. Candidates can submit videos to try to sway the response of children.

To make it more absurd, let us have it paid for and implemented by the Iowa State government.

That is known as the Iowa Youth Straw Poll.[166] The state of Iowa conducts it to teach students about the presidential election process, which is a laudable aim as Iowa has an outsized role in these elections. Yet, the media also covers the results of this student poll.

Critics can make legitimate arguments that polls have become too influential. At the least, it should be *real* polls doing the influencing. It is shocking that the media would be interested in the Iowa Straw Polls. This media attention causes candidates to pull out all stops to succeed in them, as lesser-known candidates know that failure to launch in the straw polls dooms their candidacy.

---

166 "Iowa Youth Straw Poll," Iowa.gov, accessed February 15, 2022, https://sos.iowa.gov/youth/poll/index. html.

Covering the Iowa Straw Polls has as much credibility to the election as trusting a rodent in western Pennsylvania to predict the continuation of winter by seeing his shadow. The difference is that Groundhog Day is covered as a quirky diversion in the middle of winter and not as a meteorological event. The media cover the Iowa Straw Polls as valid measures of voter interest.

The media have an insatiable appetite for polls. This need causes them to report on polls of suspect quality and sometimes lose their journalistic integrity along the way. It is up to the polling industry to stop this.

Earlier recommendations of better establishing brands and having a trusted referee can help. Poor polls receive oxygen in today's fragmented media environment. This air should not be furnished by the major networks, cable channels, newspapers, and periodicals. Their brands suffer when they report inaccurate information. It is in their self-interest to only report on polls with a sound methodology. Pollsters need to educate them.

Accepting polling standards or a referee's judgment on a poll requires media cooperation. Media organizations are large corporations in a competitive industry. It may be unrealistic to expect them to work together on anything. However, there is a relatively recent example of the media working together on polls.

Media organizations devote considerable resources to making timely election night calls. It is difficult for anyone not working in the news to understand the pressure these outlets feel to make an election call moments before their competition.

This pressure led to consternation among political scientists in the 1980 election. The 1980 contest was a landslide election with Ronald Reagan handily defeating Jimmy Carter (489 to 49 electoral votes). The media made an early call that Reagan would be the next president, prompting Carter to make a concession speech.

This early call and Carter's speech came before election sites were closed in the western time zone. Carter's concession influenced many Democratic voters to stay home in western states, which affected down-ballot races. Democratic office seekers in western states were livid with Carter.

This issue led networks to come to a tacit agreement not to call any race when there were still voters who had an opportunity to vote. This shows that major news brands can agree to do things for the common good, even in the competitive news field.

Astute viewers of election night coverage will notice news networks have become more cautious about projecting close states even when they likely have the data needed to make a call. The 2000 election caused this, as many news outlets called Florida for Al Gore and had to sheepishly recant as the result became more uncertain.

Pressure to get calls correct and make them speedily is so pronounced that on election night, news organizations have "decision desks." These are rooms of experts supported by analysts intentionally cut off from reporters. Their goal is to make election calls based on data as soon as they can be responsibly made. The desks remove the decision makers from the emotion of the situation.

In 2020, the increase in mail-in voting made election night calls precarious, and many news organizations took a week or more to call some states. News organizations were gun shy about making an incorrect call. Their analysts did not have experience in predicting results when such a large percentage of the ballots were mailed in and not counted before election night.

Ever wondered how news organizations call these races at the moment the election sites close, before election returns are tabulated? What are the people at the decision desks doing?

They are not clairvoyant: the answer is exit polling.

Exit polling is basic in principle and byzantine in practice. The United States has more than 10,000 election districts. Exit pollsters use a complex formula to designate a few hundred for exit polling. This method depends on past voter behavior, which presents the same problem the polls currently have of looking to the past to predict the future.

Consider the challenge an exit polling firm faces. They first have to select hundreds of polling locations, many in far-flung places. They have to recruit 1,000 interviewers from all over the country, train them, get them to interview voters immediately after they vote. They need to approach voters from specified demographic categories (that they need to determine by sight), tally up findings, and call results into a central phone center or type them into an online form.

It is a near-impossible task. It seems like a research miracle that this system worked well for as long as it did.

Complexity aside, exit polling is costly. At one point, America's major news organizations agreed to cooperate on them because of the expense. They needed the data, but any individual organization did not have the money to fund the exit polls.

The Voter News Service (VNS) was created in 1990 by the Associated Press, ABC, CBS, CNN, Fox News, and NBC. VNS was a consortium that pooled the exit polling resources of these organizations. It enabled them to share costs and fund an extensive exit polling effort.

On election night, VNS provided a data stream to these news organizations. The media used this stream to call election winners and provide data for analysts to discuss why people voted as they did.

Although VNS was established so news organizations could share costs, it is another example of a competitive news industry cooperating.

Major news outlets could share resources to set better polling standards, release polls on a schedule that does not interfere with the democratic process, and better fund polls. Polls deserve better funding, and pollsters need to put more resources into them than they do currently.

Why do all these major news organizations each have a polling partnership? These polls ask the same questions, use similar samples, and deploy similar LVMs. The differentiating factor is how the data are analyzed and not how they are collected.

Financial incentives can nudge news organizations in this direction. Current polling spending is inefficient. This has resulted in polls that reflect poorly on these media organizations. Banding together to conduct better polls is in their self-interest, as they will get better information. And it will cost less.

An alliance like this is fragile. VNS fell apart in 1994, when ABC News clandestinely hired a firm to conduct exit polls behind the backs of its partners. This consortium was sued for antitrust violations. The concept of shared exit polls failed because the polls were poor and suffered from technological issues. In the end, the quality of the service was not there. These would not be issues for a shared polling consortium.

IDEA 8: DISINTERMEDIATION—GO DIRECTLY TO READERS TO COMMUNICATE POLL RESULTS

Nuance is required to interpret opinion polling and pre-election polling results. The polls themselves are not complicated. Rather, the underlying public opinion they seek to measure can be sophisticated.

When polls have inconsistent results, the opinions being measured are likely complex and not distillable into a single polling question.

In corporate research, clients rarely make a consequential decision based on a single data point in a study. If the information needed for a decision could be decanted into one question, the answer would be so clear there would be no need to pay for an expensive research study in the first place.

Marketers consider many angles when designing their market

research projects. Insightful analysts search for a narrative connecting data points across many data sources.

Researchers create subtle, nuanced stories. Compelling research presentations lead to well-supported conclusions and sound decisions. Effective research presentations and reports also take between an hour and 90 minutes to make their case. This is much harder to do in a short news story.

The media are the primary distribution channel for opinion and pre-election polls. Broadcast media briefly mention poll results in the context of other stories. When given their own segment, polls are discussed in two minutes or less.

Print media provide better context and more nuanced analyses of polls. Unfortunately, newspaper and magazine readership is waning, so this nuance is being lost.

Online articles reporting poll results are getting shorter, and headlines are becoming more sensational, as online news entities' fiscal futures are more dependent on generating headline clicks than solid journalism.

The result is that the format of today's media forces the communication of polling results with little context. Public opinion is not always straightforward. Discussion of public opinion is a poor fit for current media channels.

I believe the public can understand the subtleties involved in election and opinion polling, but the current media available to them are poor conduits for this information.

Pollsters should consider taking their case to the public. They can circumvent the media by using their websites to report on polling results, hosting podcasts that provide context, and providing a resource for the press.

This idea would require a polling firm to build its own content and audience. There is precedent for this. Although not technically a polling site, FiveThirtyEight has built a considerable direct-to-consumer communication platform. FiveThirtyEight has in-depth articles, podcasts, and more, and their site discloses their methodology and provides access to their data. Their content receives significant secondary coverage from other media. FiveThirtyEight has become a trusted brand, known for pegging articles with solid data and science and contextualizing the results of their models.

And let us not forget that the early pollsters, including George Gallup and Louis Harris, communicated polling results via newsletters and syndicated columns. The pollster, not the media, dictated the context in which poll findings were shared.

Today's online environment is conducive to this happening again. Hosting a communication platform would enable the pollster to control the context, keep partisan discussions about poll results civil and fair, and become a conduit of truth. Establishing such an online portal would go a long way to building trust in polling brands and pollsters.

IDEA 9: CHANGE HOW POLLS ARE REPORTED TO HELP PEOPLE UNDERSTAND PROBABILITY

Most people, researchers and pollsters included, focus on one data point when looking at polls—the spread in the "horse race" poll. We see Biden has an eight-point lead and assume the election is in the bag. The challenge for pollsters is conveying the uncertainty around an estimate like this.

People are bad at understanding probability and risk, myself included. There are many examples of this.

Most people go through life overinsured. I read an article once that implied the average person would total one vehicle in their lifetime. Yet, the amount of car insurance they will pay for has a break-even point of totaling five cars. Even professional investors fail to account for risk correctly in their choices. Most market researchers I know play the lottery. The human brain is not designed to understand probability and risk.

I am not any better at it than anyone else, but I did have an aha moment where I understood the inability of people to value risk could lead to bizarre behavior. Economic theory has an underlying assumption that economic actors (i.e., people) behave rationally.[167] This assumption is similar to physicists assuming that we exist in a vacuum, a world without friction.

Economists believe people seek out information and rationally weigh alternatives before making choices. Choices are made rationally by people with all available information. Altruism does not exist—the only reason you would do something for

---

167 Michael C. Jensen and William H. Meckling, "The Nature of Man," *Journal of Applied Corporate Finance* 7, no. 2 (1994): 4–19, https://papers.ssrn.com/sol3/papers.cfm?abstract_id=5471.

someone else was if you derived something from it yourself. Economics is a dismal but perhaps effective way of viewing the world.

An academic paper by Daniel Kahneman and Amos Tversky[168] was required reading in the last economics course I ever took. This paper was a force behind the field of behavioral economics. It showed clear cases where individuals did not make rational decisions when factual information was in front of them. Economic theories assume people behave rationally. Kahneman and Tversky did dozens of experiments that showed people do not. The reasons seemed to be in their inability to understand probability and value risk.

I realized for the first time how inaccurate people could be at processing risk and uncertainty. Fast forward a few decades, and these concepts apply to the reporting of polling information.

Most people can understand Biden has an eight-point lead over Trump. Most cannot understand there is a 95% chance his lead lies somewhere between five and 11 points and that there is even a tiny chance Trump is leading. And that is only true if there are no errors beyond sampling errors.

That is a concept pollsters must convey because it is what this result means. It is not very clear. To the point where I bet you had to read that last paragraph more than once to understand it.

The media do not do a good job conveying uncertainty in polling. It is not an easy concept to explain.

---

168 Daniel Kahneman and Amos Tversky, "Prospect Theory: An Analysis of Decision under Risk," *Econometrica* 37, no. 2 (1979): 263–92, https://www.jstor.org/stable/1914185.

The pollsters and the media try to convey what an eight-point Biden lead means, the potential path to victory for Trump, and what the sampling error implies. All their readers hear is, "Biden is going to win."

Pollsters are frustrated by this. They do not want to be seen as bookies setting a betting line on elections. They want to be viewed as conduits of public opinion and as helping everyone understand the nuances of what drives each candidate's support.

FiveThirtyEight makes a valiant attempt to contextualize the uncertainty inherent in polls. They create probabilistic models. Instead of saying Biden has an eight-point lead nationally (which is irrelevant, as it is the swing states that matter), FiveThirtyEight will note he has an "87% chance of winning."

Even better, FiveThirtyEight uses relatable examples to communicate what an 87% chance means. By these calculations, the 2020 election prediction was about the same as rolling a six-sided die where Trump's chance of winning was the same as rolling a one, and Biden's was about the same as rolling any number between two and six.

Nate Silver tried to explain probability to the masses before the 2012 election. He wrote that "an NFL team that leads by a field goal with three minutes left to go winds up winning the game 79% of the time. These were Mr. Obama's chances in the FiveThirtyEight forecast."[169]

Probabilities are challenging to communicate because people

---

169 Nate Silver, "Oct. 31: Obama's Electoral College 'Firewall' Holding in Polls," FiveThirtyEight, November 1, 2012, https://fivethirtyeight.com/features/oct-31-obamas-electoral-college-firewall-holding-in-polls/.

see a low probability as meaning something will not happen. When my local meteorologist tells me there is a 13% chance of rain tomorrow, I leave my umbrella home and blame him when I get wet. When pollsters tell me there is a 25% chance Trump will defeat Clinton, I blame them when that unlikelihood materializes.

Pollsters could hedge and provide different estimates based on various turnout levels. Predicting turnout is complex, and it affects most pollsters' estimates. Many things beyond a pollster's control can influence turnout (early voting, Election Day weather, etc.). Pre-election polls would never miss if everyone contacted answered the survey and voter turnout was 100%. There would be no sampling error.

I can see a future where pollsters make estimates depending on whether 50%, 60%, or 70% of voters turn out for the election.

People have come to expect precision from the polls they are not capable of providing. It is unreasonable to demand certainty, as the only elections that can be predicted with 100% certainty occur in China and Russia.

Educating the media and the public on what the polls can conclude is essential. However, we need to increase the certainty around our polling estimates at the same time.

IDEA 10: RESPECT RESPONDENTS AND TREAT THEM LIKE PEOPLE

Pollsters should empathize with their future respondents when designing studies. Empathy is a skill in short supply among today's pollsters. Maybe it is because in the halcyon telephone research days, researchers would hear how they were interrupting people's lives to ask them questions. It made researchers focus on making the experience rewarding for them.

The 3,000 projects I have worked on have had an average survey length of 12 minutes, and I would estimate an average sample size of 500 people. Doing the math, this implies that people have spent approximately 300,000 hours (or 34 years) providing my clients with data.

So in an average year in my career, I have been responsible for people collectively taking a year's worth of time responding to the questionnaires I have authored.

It is crucial I see responsibility in this. People's time is precious, and I have taken up much of it as a researcher.

There has been a decline in empathy for the people who take surveys and polls. The deterioration in response rates and increased bias is related to this lack of empathy.

Researchers like to rely on intrinsic motivations from people to compel them to answer polls. People should feel that their opinions matter and that responding to a survey is a way to be heard and represent others like you.

Researchers increasingly rely on extrinsic motivations. They expect people to complete polls because they get paid to do so.

Market researchers and pollsters pay scant attention to respondent management. People are oversurveyed.

Researchers torture people with long questionnaires. They torment them with poorly designed questions. Panel managers at sampling firms do their best but are under pressure to monetize their panels. During internal disagreements, panel managers try to be the voice of respondents, but they lose out to the short-term business pressures.

The result is, pollsters are no longer trusted. The future of our democracy depends on the public trusting poll results. It starts with us respecting them as survey respondents.

Let us view the individuals who take surveys as "people" instead of "respondents." Let us give panel managers more say in how the panels are used. Let us have market research industry groups convene to discuss the need for trust. Researchers should track respondent trust and share success stories.

Researchers have polluted the national respondent base over time. We need to clean it up and reestablish trust.

CONCLUSION

I was fortunate to take a course from an unforgettable business law professor. What he chose to do with his last lecture became the most memorable moment in my academic training.

He began by stating that our final session would not relate to business law. We were to drop our pens and not take notes. We should just listen. The content of this lecture would not be on the final exam.

He predicted that 20 or 30 years down the road, we would not recall much about his class or what we had learned in the MBA program. So he declared that he would conclude with a lecture on a topic we would never forget, one that, as future business leaders, we should return to in times of uncertainty.

The lecture was on the value of simplicity.

He began by presenting case studies of some of the most influential leaders in history—trailblazers like Jesus of Nazareth, the Buddha, Genghis Khan, Galileo, Isaac Newton, Napoleon, Abraham Lincoln, and Gandhi.

One by one, he described deeply human moments where each of these leaders faced complex issues and when people surrounding them were suggesting intricate solutions. Their success as leaders was that they were steadfast in their goals and could cut through complexity and see the simplicity in front of them. They saw the signal through the noise.

He provided many examples.

Jesus masterfully boiled down the Bible's complexity to two sentences when scribes asked what the greatest part of the Jewish law was. At the time, the Jewish law contained more than 600 different regulations. It was confusing to citizens (most of whom were illiterate) as well as the clergy. The scribes were trying to trap him into misinterpreting the law.

Jesus distilled this complexity masterfully when he replied:

> "Love the Lord your God with all your heart and with all your soul and with all your mind." This is the first and greatest command-ment. And the second is like it: "Love your neighbor as yourself." All the Law and the Prophets hang on these two commandments.[170]

That was it. Two rules to live by from which all other rules are derived.

Galileo's contribution to scientific thought was as much about

---

170 Matthew 22:36–40, New International Version.

simplicity as theorizing that the Earth revolves around the sun. He rejected complex views about the solar system. He famously wrote that "nature does not multiply things unnecessarily."

Abraham Lincoln assembled a team of rivals[171] as his advisors. He kept his goal of preserving the Union forefront in his mind as he led these rivals to support simple solutions to complex problems. Lincoln was a master of simplicity and timing, as he knew how to stir a pot of complexity and wait for it to settle. Lincoln did not ignore conflict and complexity—he incited it. But he also knew when to distill a conflict to its bare roots.

Albert Einstein famously boiled down the complex concept of special relativity to an equation with three terms ($E = mc^2$).[172] An intricate problem had a simple and elegant solution that eluded other scientists for decades.

Three terms to explain the universe? A solution cannot get more parsimonious than that.

Gandhi was not born into a life of simplicity. He became an unassuming, uncomplicated man who took decades to develop his philosophy, only to realize that the truth in front of him was omnipresent and straightforward. It merely needed to be noticed. He mused, "I have nothing new to teach the world. Truth and nonviolence are as old as the hills."

To Gandhi, answers to vexing problems were a matter of tuning into the world's core simplicity.

---

171 Doris Kearns Goodwin, *Team of Rivals: The Political Genius of Abraham Lincoln* (New York: Simon & Schuster, 2006).

172 Actually, two terms, as the speed of light is a constant.

"You will discover," said my professor, "that when times get hectic, the 'experts' around you will try to show how ingenious they are by proposing complex solutions. If you learn anything in this course or business school, I want it to be that value lies in simplicity. If a problem looks intractable, it means you are not asking the right questions to begin with, or you are considering complex solutions for no reason. Always remember that simplicity is the ultimate sophistication."

He was right. It is the one lesson I learned in business school that has rung truest throughout my career.

A principle in science known as Occam's razor implies that problems should be solved using the simplest, most economical solution possible. Scientists use this heuristic to favor the simpler solution when confronted with competing theories.

When in doubt, simplify.

In *The Wizard of Oz*, Dorothy and her dog, Toto, land in the dreamland of Oz. Their circuitous journey leads them to the Wizard—an omnipotent man who can make everything right with the aid of some complex machinery. They look to the Wizard to make things better. He has a mystical, booming presence and an unquestioned authority.

Dorothy implores the Wizard to take her back to her home. The Wizard obfuscates and refuses to deliver Dorothy to her world.

At Dorothy's apex of frustration, Toto reveals the great, powerful Wizard of Oz to be a mere man. The Wizard is hiding behind a curtain and smoke and mirrors. Despite perceptions, he has no power to make things right.

All is not lost for Dorothy and Toto, as they realize the power they needed to get home was within them all along. It just needed to be recognized. With a few taps of the ruby slippers, Dorothy is back in Kansas.

Pollsters and methodologists are not wizards and hold no extraordinary power. They are intelligent and well-meaning but not all-powerful. Pollsters fail to see that the ability to improve their work is within them (and not their methodologists). They need to get rid of the smoke and mirrors and make their work simple and explainable.

Polling problems seem intractable, complex, and self-inflicted. Pollsters favor intricate theories and problematic assumptions to explain polling misfires. Layering assumptions and including more variables in analyses make pollsters look sharp but provide more opportunities for things to go wrong.

And they have—throughout the history of modern polling, and especially in the elections of 2012, 2016, and 2020.

The path to improving the polls lies in stepping back and recognizing the simplicity of what is being done. Sometimes less is more. We may not want second graders to develop our solutions, but they should understand them.

Polls are basic. Pollsters ask a few people whom they will vote for and assume others will answer the same way.

Let us stop getting cute with how we pose questions. Asking whom a person will vote for and if they plan on voting is not a complicated task.

Let us stop making samples look random and treating them as if they are when they are not. Instead, let us focus our energy around the representativeness of the samples we can get. Why care about random samples in the first place? Because random samples make it possible to know what a broader population thinks. On the sampling side, let us have methodologists concentrate on the right problem. Pollsters have convenience samples and need them to be predictive of the voting population.

Let us stop listening to methodologists yammer on about likely voter models (LVMs). These models are backward-looking, overcomplicated, and hidden from scrutiny. Which all would be fine, except scant evidence exists that LVMs work.

Instead, let us simplify. Let us trust people to tell us if they will take the time to vote.

Let us stop modeling the past. If you gave me historical stock market data, I guarantee I could develop a statistical model that precisely predicted yesterday's stock price of any given stock. This does not mean that I know what that stock's price will be tomorrow. Learning from the mistakes of 2016 and 2020 does not have to lead to the development of complex models that predict those past elections.

Instead of trusting the methodologists, let us trust poll takers to tell us what they will do in the future. Let us treat them as people and not data points to make this happen. Let us make it easy for them to take part in our surveys.

Let us not move forward by assuming our problem is we are misunderstood—that people are simply not understanding the uncertainty in what we do as pollsters. Let us get better at what we do.

More than anything else, as an industry, market researchers and pollsters need to develop greater trust with respondents. They are the lifeblood of our field, and researchers treat them poorly.

Let us pressure our associations and polling firms to invest in improving trust among poll takers rather than commencing endless seminars where methodologists machinate over statistical nuances. Increasing respondent trust will result in better information.

Let us imagine a world where every person contacted agreed to participate in a pre-election poll and gave thoughtful answers to each question. Polls would be accurate.

Well, 19 out of 20 times at least.

ACKNOWLEDGMENTS

This book was perhaps more improbable than Trump's 2016 electoral victory. I am not a pollster nor a writer and did not set out to write a book on the polls.

After the 2020 election, I started worrying about how the damaging PR election polls were getting would negatively impact my research company since polls and market research use the same methods. I decided to compose a few short blog posts on the subject because I was getting peppered with questions from clients and friends.

This led me down a rabbit hole of learning more about the pre-election polls, their problems, and this book. I wrote it because, although I am not a polling expert, my survey research experience affords me a unique perspective. I conduct dozens of studies each year that use the same methods as the polls, and I know how the sausage is made.

I have a vested interest in the polls getting better but have nothing riding on the current methods of conducting them. I have pollster friends but am not shy about criticizing their work. To a person, even those who have created and perfected the methods I critique, these friends encouraged me to publish this book.

If I have learned anything in my career, it is that success is as much due to being lucky in having the right people around you as anything else. You rarely get to thank these people publicly, and here is my chance. Please note that the content in this book and its errors are mine only, but you can blame these people for having a formative influence on me!

First, I have to thank Professor Ronald Yeaple, who encouraged me to consider a career in market research when he taught me at the MBA program at the University of Rochester. I may have never discovered the field without him.

I started my research firm because I thought I was incapable of working for someone else. In retrospect, I can see that it was because I cannot conceive of working for anyone better than the first two bosses and mentors I had: Betti Abbas and Gordon S. Black.

Crux Research would not have survived if not for the great people we have had work for and with us—especially Lisa Chen, Sue Geraci, Maureen Palmerini, and Nan Burgess-Whitman.

Our clients have been amazing, and I have learned so much from them. I still cannot believe I got paid to work with these people. Thanks to all of you.

I want to thank the researchers who were kind enough to comment on my drafts. I know you did not agree with everything

I have to say. Because they are currently working in research and polling firms, they have to remain nameless.

Thanks to the pollsters and research insiders who agreed to be interviewed for this book. Some of you did not know me in advance, yet you blessed me with your time and candor.

Thanks to FiveThirtyEight and RealClearPolitics for making the polling data for recent elections accessible.

Thanks to those who proofread drafts intending to keep me from embarrassing myself, especially Kerry Edelstein. A special thanks to George Terhanian, who unwittingly became my sounding board for this book and commented on early drafts. His modeling of the Crux Poll data uncovered many insights.

A special thanks to my wife, Sue. It would take an entire book to express my appreciation to you, so I will just leave it there.

A heartfelt thank-you to my mother, who passed away as this book was in the editing stage. You literally gave me everything unconditionally. You taught me all my words, but there are none to express how much I miss you.

The stories in this book are true, with a few names hidden and details changed to protect the innocent.

I would like to thank Winnebago Industries, as most of this book was composed while living the van life in a Class B Travato amid some of the most beautiful landscapes in the United States. Finally, I would also like to thank Bob Dylan, whose music was my constant companion and has given me faith that true genius can exist.

Did this book help you think about polls differently? If so, I would love to hear about it. Honest reviews help readers find the right book for their needs. Please consider reviewing this book on Amazon or other outlets.

ABOUT THE AUTHOR

JOHN GERACI is the founder and president of Crux Research, a market research agency located in New York. He has overseen nearly two million interviews and more than three thousand survey research projects for nonprofits, public school districts, colleges/universities, technology firms, consumer packaged goods companies, advertising agencies, media, manufacturers, and dot-com businesses.

John has been interviewed by CNN, NPR, *The New York Times*, *The Washington Post*, *The Wall Street Journal*, *USA Today*, and other media outlets such as Ad Week and Advertising Age. He has presented at more than seventy-five industry events and symposia. Learn more at cruxresearch.com.

BIBLIOGRAPHY

Asher, Herbert. *Polling and the Public: What Every Citizen Should Know*. Washington, DC: CQ Press, 2016.

Bethlehem, J. *Understanding Public Opinion Polls*. Abingdon, UK: CRC Press, 2017.

Bishop, George F. *The Illusion of Public Opinion: Fact and Artifact in American Public Opinion Polls*. Lanham, MD: Rowman & Littlefield, 2004.

Black, Gordon S., and Benjamin D. Black. *The Politics of American Discontent: How a New Party Can Make Democracy Work Again*. Hoboken, NJ: Wiley, 1994.

Bradburn, N. M., S. Sudman, B. Wansink, and N. M. Bradburn. *Asking Questions: The Definitive Guide to Questionnaire Design— for Market Research, Political Polls, and Social and Health Questionnaires*. Chichester, UK: Wiley, 2004.

Bryce, James. *The American Commonwealth, Vol. 2.* Indianapolis: Liberty Fund, 1888.

Campbell, W. J. *Lost in a Gallup: Polling Failure in US Presidential Elections.* Oakland: University of California Press, 2020.

Churchill, Gilbert A., and Dawn Iacobucci. *Marketing Research: Methodological Foundations.* Nashville: South Western Educational Publishing, 2006.

Eisinger, R. M. *The Evolution of Presidential Polling.* Cambridge: Cambridge University Press, 2003.

Goidel, Kirby, ed. *Political Polling in the Digital Age: The Challenge of Measuring and Understanding Public Opinion.* Baton Rouge: Louisiana State University Press, 2011.

Goodwin, Doris Kearns. *Team of Rivals: The Political Genius of Abraham Lincoln.* New York: Simon & Schuster, 2006.

Groves, Robert M., Floyd J. Fowler Jr., Mick P. Couper, James M. Lepkowski, Eleanor Singer, and Roger Tourangeau. *Survey Methodology.* Vol. 561. Hoboken, NJ: Wiley, 2011.

Harris, Louis. *The Anguish of Change.* New York: Norton, 1973.

Herbst, Susan. *Numbered Voices: How Opinion Polling Has Shaped American Politics.* Chicago: University of Chicago Press, 1995.

Igo, S. E. *The Averaged American: Surveys, Citizens, and the Making of a Mass Public.* Cambridge, MA: Harvard University Press, 2009.

Kahneman, Daniel. *Thinking, Fast and Slow*. New York: Farrar, Straus and Giroux, 2011.

Kahneman, Daniel, Paul Slovic, and Amos Tversky, eds. *Judgment under Uncertainty: Heuristics and Biases*. New York: Cambridge University Press, 1982.

Larsen, Erik Gahner, and Zoltán Fazekas. *Reporting Public Opinion: How the Media Turns Boring Polls into Biased News*. New York: Springer Nature, 2021.

Lichtman, Allan J. *Predicting the Next President: The Keys to the White House*. Lanham, MD: Rowman & Littlefield, 2020.

Mlodinow, Leonard. *The Drunkard's Walk: How Randomness Rules Our Lives*. New York: Pantheon, 2008.

Moore, David William. *The Opinion Makers: An Insider Exposes the Truth behind the Polls*. Boston: Beacon, 2008.

Moore, David William. *The Superpollsters: How They Measure and Manipulate Public Opinion in America*. New York: Four Walls Eight Windows, 1992.

Mosteller, Frederick. "The Pre-election Polls of 1948: Report to the Committee on Analysis of Pre-election Polls and Forecasts." *American Journal of Sociology* 56, no. 2 (1950): 200–2.

Newport, Frank. *Polling Matters: Why Leaders Must Listen to the Wisdom of the People*. New York: Grand Central Publishing, 2004.

Rae, S. F., and G. Gallup. *The Pulse of Democracy; The Public-Opinion Poll and How It Works*. New York: Greenwood, 1968.

Rank, Michael. *How Iowa Conquered the World: The Story of a Small Farm State's Journey to Global Dominance*. Kansas City, MO: Five Minute Books, 2014.

Robinson, Matthew. *Mobocracy: How the Media's Obsession with Polling Twists the News, Alters Elections, and Undermines Democracy*. Shreveport, LA: Prima, 2002.

Rushkoff, D. *Present Shock: When Everything Happens Now*. London: Penguin, 2013.

Salvanto, Anthony. *Where Did You Get This Number? A Pollster's Guide to Making Sense of the World*. New York: Simon & Schuster, 2019.

Scipione, Paul. *A Nation of Numbers: The Development of Marketing Research in America*. St. Paul, MN: Quirks Market Research Media, 2015.

Seltzer, *Richard A. US Public Opinion since the 1930s: Galluping through History*. Washington, DC: Rowman & Littlefield, 2022.

Silver, Nate. *The Signal and the Noise: Why So Many Predictions Fail—but Some Don't*. London: Penguin, 2012.

Surowiecki, J. *The Wisdom of Crowds: Why the Many Are Smarter than the Few and How Collective Wisdom Shapes Business, Economies, Societies and Nations*. Palatine, IL: Anchor Books, 2005.

Thaler, Richard H., and Cass R. Sunstein. *Nudge: The Final Edition.*
London: Penguin, 2021.

Tocqueville, Alexis de. *Democracy in America.* London: Saunders
and Otley, 2003.

Traugott, Michael W., and Paul J. Lavrakas. *The Voter's Guide to
Election Polls.* Morrisville, NC: Lulu, 2016.

Warren, Kenneth F. *In Defense of Public Opinion Polling.* Abingdon,
UK: Routledge, 2002.

Wheeler, Michael. *Lies, Damn Lies, and Statistics: The Manipulation
of Public Opinion in America.* New York: Norton, 1976.

Zakaria, Fareed. *Ten Lessons for a Post-pandemic World.* London:
Penguin, 2020.

Made in the USA
Las Vegas, NV
20 September 2022

55666813R00184